SUNĀMA
BEAUTIFUL SANSKRIT NAMES

Sunāma

Beautiful Sanskrit Names

Nityānanda Miśra

BLOOMSBURY
NEW DELHI • LONDON • OXFORD • NEW YORK • SYDNEY

BLOOMSBURY INDIA
Bloomsbury Publishing India Pvt. Ltd
Second Floor, LSC Building No. 4, DDA Complex, Pocket C – 6 & 7,
Vasant Kunj New Delhi 110070

BLOOMSBURY, BLOOMSBURY INDIA and the Diana logo are trademarks of Bloomsbury Publishing Plc

First published in India 2021
This edition published 2021

Tree Vectors by Vecteezy

ISBN: TPB: 978-9-3903-5810-6; eBook: 978-9-3903-5826-7

16 15 14 13

Typeset in Charis SIL and Chanakya Sanskrit by Nityānanda Miśra

Printed and bound in India by Gopsons Papers Pvt. Ltd., Noida

FSC www.fsc.org MIX Paper | Supporting responsible forestry FSC® C191020 like Vedas, *Purāṇas*, *Rāmāyaṇa*, *Mahābhārata*, *koṣas*, and *sahasranāmas*. This book is also different from other books on Sanskrit or Hindu names in that most names in this book are rare. I have used less than 50 results on LinkedIn (which has more than six crore Indians) on a first name search as a benchmark for rarity. Most names in this book have fewer than 50 search results on LinkedIn. Exceptions include some names which are popular outside India or among non-Hindus, but are also Sanskrit names. For example, 'Sara' is well-known to be an Abrahamic name but few people know that it is also a Sanskrit name—the epithet *sārā* (सारा) is used for Durgā in the *Devī Māhātmya* of the *Mārkaṇḍeya-Purāṇa*. For such names, I have used my discretion instead of the number of search results on LinkedIn. The opposite gender versions may not be as rare in all cases, they have been given for the sake of completeness.

For writing this book, I read more than 70,000 names from the aforementioned sources. The book has around 1,700 names (around 3,100 names including the opposite gender entries) drawn from as many as seventy-seven Sanskrit texts, including thirty eight *sahasranāmas*. Most names are from *sahasranāmas* and *Purāṇas*, and a lot of names from *kośas* and Vedic texts that I shortlisted could not be included in this edition due to time constraints and page guidelines from the publisher. I hope to include them in future editions of this book.

I have made my best efforts to keep this book error-free. Still, if any errors have remained in the draft, I request readers

To Ṛṣi Vasiṣṭha

यस्मिन् रमन्ते मुनयः स रामो
ददौ वसिष्ठो हरये सुनाम

"In whom *munis* rejoice—he is *Rāma*,
To him, Vasiṣṭha gave a *sunāma*."

Preface

Bhārata, also known as India, is the land of *sunāmas* or "beautiful names". Perhaps no other language in the world can claim the vast diversity of beautiful names that Sanskrit, India's cultural fountainhead, has. It is not a surprise that the Vedic people had up to four names, as a mantra in the *Ṛgveda-Saṃhitā* (8.80.9) tells us. Commenting on the mantra, Ācārya Sāyaṇa explains that the four names included a *nakṣatra* name (based on the birth constellation or star), a *guhya* name (a secret name known to only a few people like the parents), a *prakāśa* name (the public name), and a *yajñiya* name (an epithet or title given later in life based on certain achievements). In ancient Bhārata, people had several types of names including given names, patronymics, matronymics, *gotra* names, etc. The *avātara* Rāma, the hero of the *Rāmāyaṇa*, was also known as *Dāśarathi* ("son of Daśaratha"), *Kausalyeya* ("son of Kausalyā"), and *Rāghava* ("descendant of Raghu"). The *nāmakaraṇa* or naming ceremony was an important rite with various *Gṛhya-Sūtras* listing elaborate rules and guidelines for naming a child. As an example, most *Gṛhya-Sūtras* recommended a name with an even number of syllables for a boy and an odd number of syllables for a girl. It was recommended that a name start with a sonant, contain a semi-vowel, and end with a *visarga* or a long vowel. Naming a child was thus not only an art, but also a science with its own discipline.

Names in ancient Bhārata

A name was often based on unique features of the child, circumstances surrounding the birth, or the qualities desired in the child. For example, Kālidāsa describes how King Dilīpa named his son in the *Raghuvaṃśa* (3.21), "[Thinking,] 'May this child reach the end of the scriptures and similarly [reach the end of] his enemies,' the king—conversant with meanings—named his son *Raghu*, knowing that the root [of Raghu] means 'to go'." The root of the word *raghu* is √*lagh* which means "to go" or "to reach". The word *raghu* (a variant of the word *laghu* as per the *Mahābhāṣya*) literally means "he who moves [swiftly or quickly]." Kālidāsa tells us that the name *Raghu* connoted deep meanings like "he who masters *śāstras*" and "he who defeats his enemies".

There was a time in Bhārata when almost every name was a *sunāma*. Every name had a mathematical *vyutpatti* (a scientific derivation) or an insightful *nirukti* or *nirvacana* (a mystic explanation). This tree of *sunāmas* in Bhārata, with its root in the Vedas, fructified with its sweetest fruits in the *Itihāsa* and *Purāṇa* texts which contain many *sahasranāmas* with one thousand (or 1,008) names of a single deity denoting his or her qualities or acts. These *sahasranāmas*, especially the *Viṣṇu-Sahasranāma* and the *Lalitā-Sahasranāma*, are used as sources for baby names even today in traditional Hindu families. The evergreen tree of *sunāmas* is not restricted to Hinduism, but also present in Jainism and Buddhism.

Preface

The *Amarakoṣa* lists eighteen names of Jina or Buddha and seven of Śākyamuni. Like the Hindu *sahasranāmas*, there are Jain *sahasranāmas* too, for example the *Arhan-nāmasahasra-samuccaya* and the *Pārśvanātha-Sahasranāma.*

Traditionally, a *kulaguru* or a family elder well-versed in Sanskrit would give a *sunāma* to a new-born. As per the *Rāmāyaṇa* (1.18.21–22), Vasiṣṭha gave the names Rāma, Bharata, Lakṣmaṇa, and Śatrughna to the sons of Daśaratha on the twelfth day following their birth. Similarly, as per the *Garga-Saṃhitā* (1.15.25–34), Garga gave the names Kṛṣṇa and Balarāma to the sons of Nanda.

The tradition of *sunāmas*—beautiful and meaningful Sanskrit names—continued in Bhārata even as the use of Sanskrit declined with time. There are *sunāmas* in other Indian languages too, for example the name *Arumugam* ("six-faced", i.e. Kārttikeya) in Tamil or the name *Chulbuli* ("she who is playful") in Hindi. However, Sanskrit names still hold a charm as they are not restricted to any region or language and are widely understood across India even today. Many parents in India (especially Hindus and Jains) desire to have a Sanskrit name for their child. Last year, I suggested some names to a Sikh mother who wanted a pure Sanskrit name (and not its *tadbhava* version) for her son.

Why I wrote this book

I have been studying Sanskrit for many years. All these years, I had never thought I would write a book on Sanskrit names. In this information age, when almost all the popular Sanskrit dictionaries are easily accessible on the Internet, who would need a book for Sanskrit names? It turns out that the amount of misinformation about Sanskrit names available on the Internet is so vast that a book like this needed.

In 2015, I was standing in a queue for school admissions for my son. In front of me was another parent with his daughter. When I asked the girl her name, she said "Saanvi". Her father told me that it was a Sanskrit word and a name of goddess Lakshmi. I merely smiled, as I did not want to disappoint him by telling him it was not. I later came to know that Saanvi was one of the most popular new-age names and the myth that it was a Sanskrit name for Lakshmi was quite widespread. Over the past five years, my children, named Nilaya (*nilayā*, which means "she who is the abode [of virtues]") and Niramaya (*nirāmaya*, a name of Śiva which means "he who is without [physical and mental] illnesses") introduced me to their many friends named Vivaan, Saanvi, Kiyaan, Ishanvi, etc. Many such new-age names are claimed to be Sanskrit names but they are not. These "fake Sanskrit names" are present on popular name websites which ascribe all sorts of imaginary meanings to such non-Sanskrit names. These websites pass inappropriate Sanskrit words like 'Shleshma' (*śleṣmā*, "mucus, phlegm") and 'Mehan' (*mehana*, "urination, urine, penis"), words from other languages (including Arabic, Persian, Greek, Japanese, etc.), meaningless portmanteaus like 'Krishiv' (from Krishna and Shiv), and even typos like 'Yashvasin' for 'Yashasvin' (*yaśasvin*) as Sanskrit names, often with positive but non-existent meanings. Highly-educated parents, including IIT and IIM graduates, trust these websites blindly when looking for a Sanskrit name for their soon-to-be-born or new-born children. In 2018, I started dispelling falsehoods about these fake Sanskrit names on social media. Encouraged by the response, I started exposing more and more *kunāmas* ("bad names") and parallelly started suggesting *sunāmas* ("good names") on social media. In the process I discovered that the misinformation about Sanskrit names is not restricted to name websites alone, it pervades news websites, Wikipedia, Facebook, Twitter, and even Google's featured snippets. A lot of this content is user-generated and driven by a need of parents to have a modern-sounding or an uncommon name for their child. While such is the case of the Internet, even some bestselling books on Hindu names have mistakes. As an example, *The Penguin Book of Hindu Names for Boys* lists *Hrīmān* meaning "dispeller of sorrow, wealthy" [sic], *Hulās* meaning "jubilation" [sic] and *Hurditya* meaning "joyous, happy" [sic] as "Sanskrit names" on the same page. The facts—*hrīmān* means "modest" or "ashamed" in Sanskrit, *hulās* (हुलास) is a Hindi word and not a Sanskrit word, and there is no such word as *hurditya* in Sanskrit. Last year, I delivered a talk titled "How not to name your child" where I covered these issues in addition to some generic issues with modern Sanskrit names like spelling and gender anomalies. In addition, due to lack of time and a flood of requests from parents and business owners, I started providing professional consultancy services for Sanskrit names. During the last fifteen months or so, I have validated or suggested thousands of names for hundreds of parents. Meanwhile, many well-wishers and followers on social media requested me to write a book on good Sanskrit names in order to provide parents with an authentic source for uncommon and meaningful Sanskrit names. When I came back from a one-year break from book-writing this year, I decided to take up this project.

Modern anomalies

In addition to dispelling misinformation on Sanskrit names, I also attempt to address certain anomalies seen in Sanskrit names today. One of the most widespread anomalies is the schwa syncope (deletion of the final *a* vowel) in Sanskrit words, almost ubiquitous in northern and western India. The masculine name *Rāma* is rarely pronounced and written correctly in India today, it is almost universally pronounced as *rām* and written as Ram. The phenomenon is catching up in southern and eastern India also, take for examples the names of the Tamil editor N. Ram and the Bengali politician Mukul Roy. Still, every now and then I see names being spelt as Vikrama (or Vikraman) and Garga in southern and eastern India, just how the names *vikrama* and *garga* should be spelt. I advise parents to spell and pronounce names with the terminal vowel, even if it may come at the cost of a confusion to readers who are not used to reading or hearing names with the terminal schwa. I try to follow this myself to the extent possible. My name in my passport is spelt *Nityanand*, but I spell it as *Nityananda* (the closest correct spelling for *nityānanda*) wherever possible—in my books, in my emails, and on social media.

Another widespread anomaly is the *ph* (फ) sound in many Sanskrit names being written and pronounced as *f* (फ़) and similarly the *jh* (झ) sound being written and pronounced as *z* (ज़). The *anusvāra* is often written (and pronounced) as 'n' (e.g. 'Hans' for *haṃsa*) instead of being written as 'm' (e.g. in 'Hamsa', a more accurate spelling for *haṃsa*). Parents are advised to avoid these inaccurate spellings and pronunciations and stick to spellings with 'ph', 'jh', and 'm'.

In southern India, the Sanskrit consonant त् is often spelt as 'th' and similarly द् as 'dh', while 't' and 'd' are often reserved for ट् and ड् respectively. In other parts of the country, 't' is used for both त् and ट् and similarly 'd' for both द् and ड्, while the spellings 'th' and 'dh' are used for the consonants थ् and ध् respectively. This creates confusion at times, since 'th' and 'dh' are also used for थ् and ध् respectively in the South. For example, a person in the South with the Sanskrit name *dharmada* (धर्मद, "the bestower of *dharma* or virtues") is likely to spell his name in English as 'Dharmadha' or 'Dharmadh' (there are two persons with the name 'Dharmadh' on LinkedIn), with the first 'dh' in the name standing for ध् and second for द्. While no convention can be deemed correct or incorrect as the twenty-six letters of the English alphabet are insufficient to represent all Sanskrit sounds, I recommend using 't' and 'd' for त् and द् respectively to avoid confusion. In addition, this practice is closer to the International Alphabet for Sanskrit Transliteration (IAST).

In this book, I give both Devanagari and IAST spellings for names, and leave the final Roman spelling to the discretion of the parents or the users.

A lot of gender anomalies are also seen in Sanskrit names these days, often due to the difference in genders of a word in Sanskrit and other Indian languages. Many masculine Sanskrit words like *rāśi*, *garimā*, *nidhi*, *kiraṇa*, and *tejasvī* are used as names for girls. Of these, the first four are feminine in Hindi while the last is both masculine and feminine. Many neuter Sanskrit words like *vyoma* and *tejas* are used as names for boys—these words are masculine in Hindi (which does not have a neuter gender). Sometimes, a Sanskrit word does not have a masculine or feminine equivalent, but parents still change a word and use it for the other gender. An example is Isheeka (*iṣīkā*, a feminine word in Sanskrit) which was changed to Isheek (*iṣīka*, no such word is listed in traditional or modern Sanskrit dictionaries) and used for a boy, as reported by *Mathrubhumi* in August 2018. Parents looking for a *sunāma* should avoid these gender anomalies. For these reasons, I give the gender (M for masculine and F for feminine) with each name in this book. Unisex names are shown as MF. For completeness, I also show the version of the name for the opposite gender (the masculine version of a feminine name and vice versa), wherever applicable.

What's new in this book?

Many name books for Hindu or Sanskrit names are written by authors who are not well-versed in Sanskrit and contain both common and uncommon names. This book is not a list of copy-pasted entries of words and meanings from dictionaries. Most names in this book are from ancient Sanskrit texts to point them out so that they can be corrected in reprints and future editions.

Acknowledgements

My inspiration for every literary endeavour—including this book—is my guru, Jagadguru Rāmānandācārya Svāmī Rāmabhadrācārya, who gave the *sunāmas* Nilayā and Nirāmaya to my children. No words are enough to thank him. As always, I am indebted to my parents and my children who supported me wholeheartedly while I wrote this book during the lockdown. Special thanks are due to Ami Ganatra and Prachi Mishra for their constant encouragement and help without which this book could not have been completed. Finally, I am grateful to the many users of Facebook and Twitter who suggested time and again to write a book on Sanskrit names and provided valuable suggestions and feedback.

May this book help its readers find the right *sunāma* they are looking for. May the evergreen tree of *sunāmas* continue to grow and bear fruits.

Nityānanda Miśra
Mumbai, 15 August 2020

Note to the Reader

This book uses the International Alphabet of Sanskrit Transliteration (IAST) scheme to transliterate Sanskrit names and words. A transliteration key is not provided as the scheme can be easily learned from the Wikipedia page on IAST. Names are given in both Devanagari and IAST, while the eventual Roman spelling of the name is left to the discretion of the user.

Names are listed in the Devanagari alphabetical order, starting with *a* (अ) and ending with *ha* (ह). If required, this order can also be easily learned from the Wikipedia page on Devanagari. For ease of look-up, the header on each page lists the first and the last names on the page.

For names ending with a vowel sound (*ajanta* names), I list the base form or the lemma of the name (as in *viṣṇu* and *lakṣmī*) and not the inflected nominative singular form (as in *viṣṇuḥ* or *lakṣmīḥ*). Exceptions to this are names ending with the vowel *ṛ* (e.g. *anumantṛ*) for which I list the nominative singular form (e.g. *anumantā*). For names ending with a consonant sound (*halanta* names), I list the inflected form (as in *mahān*) and not the base form (as in *mahat*), except when the inflected nominative singular form involves the *visarga* in which case I list the base form (as in *aṅgiras*) and not the inflected form (as in *aṅgirāḥ*). This convention is to avoid the use of the *visarga*, which often occurs in inflected forms of Sanskrit words and names but is prone to mispronunciation and can cause confusion.

In each name entry, meaning(s) of the name is (are) given within double quotes. Often, name meanings require some context and explanations. Square brackets are used to provide the context and round brackets are used for explanations. While a lot can be written on meanings of Sanskrit names, in this book I present meanings in brief. Most meanings are in accordance with Sanskrit commentaries on the texts and/or Sanskrit grammar rules, with a few meanings presented as per the *niruktis* or *nirvacanas* for the name in Hindu scriptures.

The gender of the name is shown as M (masculine), F (feminine), or MF (both masculine and feminine, i.e. a unisex name). The opposite gender versions of names are given at the end of name entries.

The deity or person (or entity, in some cases) for whom the name has been used are given outside double quotes. In most cases, the source text where the name is used or listed is also indicated with an abbreviation. Book, chapter, and verse numbers in the source have not been given for the sake of brevity. The alphabetical list of all abbreviations used is provided at the end of the book.

Sunāma

अंशक (*aṃśaka*) M. "having a share (=a relative)", Gaṇeśa (GS2). **अंशिका** (*aṃśikā*) F.

अकल्मष (*akalmaṣa*) M. "without faults", Hanumān (HS). **अकल्मषा** (*akalmaṣā*) F.

अकामा (*akāmā*) F. "free from lust or [evil] desires", Yamunā (YS). **अकाम** (*akāma*) M.

अकाय (*akāya*) M. "without a [mortal] body", Rāma (RS1), Hanumān (HS). **अकाया** (*akāyā*) F.

अकोप (*akopa*) M. "without anger", one of Daśaratha's ministers (VR). **अकोपा** (*akopā*) F.

अक्रूर (*akrūra*) M. "not cruel", Rāma (RS1), Narasiṃha (NS). **अक्रूरा** (*akrūrā*) F. Bhavānī (BS).

अक्रोध (*akrodha*) M. "free from anger", Kṛṣṇa (KS1). **अक्रोधा** (*ukrodhā*) F.

अक्रोधन (*akrodhana*) M. "without anger, free from anger", a king (VāP). **अक्रोधना** (*akrodhanā*) F.

अक्षघ्न (*akṣaghna*) M. "the slayer of Akṣa (a son of Rāvaṇa)", Hanumān (HS). **अक्षघ्नी** (*akṣaghnī*) F.

अक्षरी (*akṣurī*) M. "having *akṣara* (=OM), reciting OM", the highest *yogī* (VāP).

अक्षोभ्य (*akṣobhya*) M. "he who cannot be perturbed", Viṣṇu (VS1), Narasiṃha (NS). **अक्षोभ्या** (*akṣobhyā*) F. Gaṅgā (GS3).

अखिन्न (*akhinna*) M. "not tired, indefatigable", Sūrya (SS1).

अखिन्ना (*akhinnā*) F.

अगद (*agada*) M. "free from [physical and mental] disease", Rāma (RS1). **अगदा** (*agadā*) F.

अगाधा (*agādhā*) F. "very deep, unfathomable", Annapūrṇā (AS), Bhavānī (BS). **अगाध** (*agādha*) M.

अगोत्रा (*agotrā*) F. "without an origin", Sītā (SS2), Pārvatī (PS). **अगोत्र** (*agotra*) M.

अग्निका (*agnikā*) F. "she who radiates like Agni", daughter of the *gandharva* leader Vikrānta (VāP). **अग्निक** (*agnika*) M.

अग्नितेजस् (*agnitejas*) MF. "having the *tejas* (brilliance) of Agni, resplendent", a *ṛṣi* (ViP).

अग्निद (*agnida*) M. "he who gives the fire (=*jñānāgni*, the fire of knowledge)", Śiva (ŚS3). **अग्निदा** (*agnidā*) F.

अग्निभास् (*agnibhās*) MF. "having the brilliance or brightness of Agni", a *deva* in Cāriṣṇava *manvantara* (VāP).

अग्निमान् (*agnimān*) M. "possessing Agni", one who maintains the sacred fire (MaP). **अग्निमती** (*agnimatī*) F.

अग्निमित्र (*agnimitra*) M. "a friend of Agni (one who performs *yajñas*)", a king (BhP), a *ṛṣi* (BhP). **अग्निमित्रा** (*agnimitrā*) F.

अग्निवर्चस् (*agnivarcas*) MF. "having the brilliance like that of Agni", a *ṛṣi* (ViP).

अग्निवर्ण (*agnivarṇa*) M. "having the complexion (brilliance) of Agni", ancestor of Rāma (VR). **अग्निवर्णा** (*agnivarṇā*) F.

अग्निशर्मा (*agniśarmā*) M. "he who destroys [*pāpa*] like Agni", a *ṛtvik* (VāP).

अग्नीध्र (*agnīdhra*) M. "he who maintains the Agni", a *ṛṣi* (BrP).

अग्रगण्य (*agragaṇya*) M. "to be counted first, the best", Rāma (RS1). अग्रगण्या (*agragaṇyā*) F.

अग्रवर (*agravara*) M. "the best among the foremost or the eminent ones", Śiva (ŚS1). अग्रवरा (*agravarā*) F.

अग्राह्य (*agrāhya*) M. "he who cannot be perceived [by the senses]", Viṣṇu (VS1). अग्राह्या (*agrāhyā*) F.

अग्र्य (*agrya*) M. "being in the front, foremost, the best", Dattātreya (DS2). अग्र्या (*agryā*) F.

अघापह (*aghāpaha*) M. "the slayer of *pāpas*", Kṛṣṇa (KS1). अघापहा (*aghāpahā*) F.

अघोर (*aghora*) M. "not terrifying, not frightening", Śiva (ŚS2). अघोरा (*aghorā*) F. Gaṅgā (GS3).

अङ्कुशा (*aṅkuśā*) F. "she who has a [distinguishing] mark or sign, she who wields the *aṅkuśa* (hook) [as a weapon]", a *śakti* (BrP). अङ्कुश (*aṅkuśa*) M.

अचञ्चल (*acañcala*) M. "steady, not wavering", Hanumān (HS). अचञ्चला (*acañcalā*) F.

अचेत्य (*acetya*) M. "not perceivable [through senses]", Dattātreya (DS2). अचेत्या (*acetyā*) F.

अजपा (*ajapā*) F. "the protector of the unborn (Brahmā)",

Gāyatrī (GS4). **अजप** (*ajapa*) M.

अजस्य (*ajasya*) M. "he who cannot be hurt or exhausted", a *ṛṣi* (MaP). **अजस्या** (*ajasyā*) F.

अञ्जिष्ठ (*añjiṣṭha*) M. "he who illuminates [the world]", a *deva* (BrP). **अञ्जिष्ठा** (*añjiṣṭhā*) F.

अणुह (*aṇuha*) M. "he who reaches (=knows) the atoms (=the minutest details)", a king (BhP). **अणुहा** (*aṇuhā*) F.

अतन्द्रित (*atandrita*) M. "not lazy, active", Śiva (ŚS1). **अतन्द्रिता** (*atandritā*) F.

अतर्क्य (*atarkya*) M. "he who cannot be comprehended through reason", Dattātreya (DS2). **अतर्क्या** (*atarkyā*) F.

अतितेजस् (*atitejas*) MF. "having extraordinary *tejas* (valour or brilliance), extremely splendid or powerful", a *ṛṣi* (BrP).

अतिनामा (*atināmā*) M. "having an extraordinary name (=fame)", a *ṛṣi* (ViP). **अतिनाम्नी** (*atināmnī*) F.

अतिबल (*atibala*) M. "very strong, a great warrior", a king (VāP). **अतिबला** (*atibalā*) F. a *mātṛkā* (MaP).

अतिभानु (*atibhānu*) MF. "with excellent rays (brilliance), extremely radiant", son of Kṛṣṇa (BhP).

अतिमान (*atimāna*) M. "of extreme measure, immeasurable", a *ṛṣi* (VāP). **अतिमाना** (*atimānā*) F.

अतिरथ (*atiratha*) M. "he who has surpassed *rathas*, an unparalleled warrior", a king (MBh). **अतिरथा** (*atirathā*) F.

अतिवीर (*atīvīra*) M. "exceedingly brave or heroic, a great hero", used for King Jayanta (MaP). **अतिवीरा** (*ativīrā*) F.

अतीन्द्रिय (*atīndriya*) M. "beyond senses", Viṣṇu (VS1), Śiva (ŚS3). **अतीन्द्रिया** (*atīndriyā*) F.

अत्युग्र (*atyugra*) M. "exceedingly fierce, very strong or mighty", Viṣṇu (VS2). **अत्युग्रा** (*atyugrā*) F.

अदीना (*adīnā*) F. "not miserable, not depressed, prosperous, cheerful, high-spirited", Yamunā (YS), Annapūrṇā (AS). **अदीन** (*adīna*) M. a king (VāP).

अद्भुता (*adbhutā*) F. "wonderful, surprising", Rādhā (RKS). **अद्भुत** (*adbhuta*) M.

अद्विषेण (*adviṣeṇa*) M. "not hateful or detestable, agreeable, desirable", a *ṛṣi* (VāP). **अद्विषेणा** (*adviṣeṇā*) F.

अधिदेव (*adhideva*) M. "the supreme *deva*", Kṛṣṇa (MBh). **अधिदेवी** (*adhidevī*) F.

अधिपति (*adhipati*) M. "a great master or ruler", son of Bhṛgu (BrP).

अधिरोह (*adhiroha*) M. "ascending, he who *bhaktas* ascend to", Śiva (ŚS1). **अधिरोहा** (*adhirohā*) F.

अधीष्ट (*adhīṣṭa*) M. "supremely desired, engaged or appointed with honour", son of Brahmā (VāP). **अधीष्टा** (*adhīṣṭā*) F.

अधृत (*adhṛta*) M. "not held, borne, or restrained [by anybody or anything], bearing everything", Viṣṇu (VS1), Śiva (ŚS3).

अधृता (*adhṛtā*) F.

अधोक्षज (*adhokṣaja*) M. "he who has subdued sensory knowledge", Viṣṇu (VS1), Rāma (RS1). **अधोक्षजा** (*adhokṣajā*) F.

अध्वग (*adhvaga*) M. "going on the [right] path", Kṛṣṇa (KS1). **अध्वगा** (*adhvagā*) F.

अध्वर्यु (*adhvaryu*) M. "he who conducts the *yajña*, knower of Yajurveda", one of the sixteen *ṛtviks* (MaP).

अध्वातीत (*adhvātīta*) M. "beyond all *adhvans* (ways)", Narasiṃha (NS). **अध्वातीता** (*adhvātītā*) F.

अनन्तजित् (*anantajit*) MF. "one who has conquered endless/infinite [enemies], all-conquering", Viṣṇu (VS1).

अनन्ताक्षी (*anantākṣī*) F. "with infinitely many eyes", Annapūrṇā (AS). **अनन्ताक्ष** (*anantākṣa*) M.

अनवद्या (*anavadyā*) F. "without blame, irreproachable", an Apsaras (VāP). **अनवद्य** (*anavadya*) M.

अनसूयक (*anasūyaka*) M. "free from envy", Rāma (RS1). **अनसूयिका** (*anasūyikā*) F. used to describe Sukanyā, the wife of Cyavana (MBh).

अनाकुल (*anākula*) M. "self-possessed, not confused", Hanumān (HS). **अनाकुला** (*anākulā*) F.

अनाद्यन्त (*anādyanta*) M. "without any beginning and without any end", Sūrya (SS1). **अनाद्यन्ता** (*anādyantā*) F.

अनाद्या (*anādyā*) F. "without any beginning, unborn", Annapūrṇā (AS), Sītā (SS2). **अनाद्य** (*anādya*) M.

अनिर्देश (*anirdeśa*) M. "he who takes no directions or orders, he who directs all", Rāma (RS1). **अनिर्देशा** (*anirdeśā*) F.

अनिर्देश्या (*anirdeśyā*) F. "she who cannot be defined or explained [completely]", Lakṣmī (LS2). **अनिर्देश्य** (*anirdeśya*) M.

अनिर्वेद्य (*anirvedya*) M. "he who cannot be known [completely], he who cannot be made despondent", Kṛṣṇa (KS1). **अनिर्वेद्या** (*anirvedyā*) F.

अनिलाभ (*anilābha*) M. "like the wind", Śiva (ŚS1). **अनिलाभा** (*anilābhā*) F.

अनीह (*anīha*) M. "without [worldly] wishes", a king (BhP). **अनीहा** (*anīhā*) F.

अनुकृष्ण (*anukṛṣṇa*) M. "he who follows Kṛṣṇa", a *ṛṣi* (BrP). **अनुकृष्णा** (*anukṛṣṇā*) F.

अनुगा (*anugā*) F. "she who follows [the right path]", Yamunā (YS). **अनुग** (*anuga*) M.

अनुतप्ता (*anutaptā*) F. "heated (=tested) again", a river (BrP, VāP). **अनुतप्त** (*anutapta*) M.

अनुत्तम (*anuttama*) M. "he who has no superior, the best, excellent", Viṣṇu (VS1), Rāma (RS1). **अनुत्तमा** (*anuttamā*) F. Lalitā (LS1).

अनुत्तर (*anuttara*) M. "having no superior, the best, excellent", Sūrya (SS1). **अनुत्तरा** (*anuttarā*) F. Rādhā (RS2).

अनुमति (*anumati*) MF. "following one's intellect", daughter of Aṅgīras and Śraddhā (BhP), a *ṛṣi* (MaP).

अनुमन्ता (*anumantā*) M. "he who consents or permits", a *deva* (BrP), an aspect of the supreme *puruṣa* (BG). **अनुमन्त्री** (*anumantrī*) F.

अनेनस् (*anenas*) MF. "without any faults", a king (BhP).

अनौपम्या (*anaupamyā*) F. "she who has no likeness or resemblance, incomparable, unparalleled, unique", Lakṣmī (LS2). **अनौपम्य** (*anaupamya*) M.

अनौषध (*anauṣadha*) M. "without medication, ever-healthy", Śiva (ŚS1). **अनौषधा** (*anauṣadhā*) F.

अन्तक (*antaka*) M. "he who causes the end [of beings at the time of *pralaya*]", Viṣṇu (VS1). **अन्तिका** (*antikā*) F.

अन्तर्धान (*antardhāna*) M. "concealed, hidden", a king (BhP). **अन्तर्धानी** (*antardhānī*) F.

अन्तर्वेद्या (*antarvedyā*) F. "to be known or experienced internally", Lakṣmī (LS2). **अन्तर्वेद्य** (*antarvedya*) M.

अन्वता (*anvatā*) F. "she who follows [the right path]", an Apsaras (VāP). **अन्वत** (*anvata*) M.

अपचिति (*apaciti*) F. "[possessing] worship, honour, respect", daughter of Marīci (VāP).

अपरार्क (*aparārka*) M. "another Sūrya (=very brilliant)", name of a commentator on *Yājñavalkya-Smṛti.*

अपस्या (*apasyā*) F. "skilled in *apas* (=action), active, skilful", used for Āpas goddesses (ŚYM). **अपस्य** (*apasya*) M.

अपार्य (*apārya*) M. "endless, he who cannot be crossed", a Rudra (BrP). **अपार्या** (*apāryā*) F.

अप्यय (*apyaya*) M. "the location of disappearance [during *pralaya*]", Viṣṇu (VS1). **अप्यया** (*apyayā*) F.

अप्रतर्क्य (*apratarkya*) M. "not to be known by reason", Kṛṣṇa (KS2), Gaṇeśa (GS2). **अप्रतर्क्या** (*apratarkyā*) F.

अप्रतिरथ (*apratiratha*) M. "without a rival charioteer, an invincible warrior", a king (BhP). **अप्रतिरथा** (*apratirathā*) F.

अप्रतिहता (*apratihatā*) F. "unimpeded, unimpaired", Lakṣmī (LS2). **अप्रतिहत** (*apratihata*) M.

अप्रपञ्च (*aprapañca*) M. "without deceit or fraud", Hanumān (HS). **अप्रपञ्चा** (*aprapañcā*) F.

अप्रमाद (*apramāda*) M. "careful, attentive, cautious", carefulness personified as the son of intellect or Buddhi (BrP). **अप्रमादा** (*apramādā*) F.

अप्रमित (*apramita*) M. "not measured, immeasurable", Narasiṃha (NS). **अप्रमिता** (*apramitā*) F.

अबाध्य (*abādhya*) M. "he who cannot be obstructed or restrained", Dattātreya (DS2). **अबाध्या** (*abādhyā*) F.

अब्जजा (*abjajā*) F. "born form the lotus", Annapūrṇā (AS). **अब्जज** (*abjaja*) M. Brahmā (TK).

अब्धिजा (*abdhijā*) F. "born from the ocean", Annapūrṇā (AS). **अब्धिज** (*abdhija*) M.

अभङ्गुर (*abhaṅgura*) M. "imperishable", Kṛṣṇa (KS1). **अभङ्गुरा** (*abhaṅgurā*) F.

अभयङ्कर (*abhayaṅkara*) M. "not frightening", Kṛṣṇa (KS2). **अभयङ्करी** (*abhayaṅkarī*) F.

अभयद (*abhayada*) M. "he who gives *abhaya* (an assurance of protection)", a king (ViP). **अभयदा** (*abhayadā*) F.

अभिगम्य (*abhigamya*) M. "easily obtainable (=knowable)", Śiva (ŚS1). **अभिगम्या** (*abhigamyā*) F.

अभिभू (*abhibhū*) MF. "one who is victorious or prosperous", Viṣṇu (MBh).

अभिमत (*abhimata*) M. "desired from all sides, agreeable", Sūrya (SS1). **अभिमता** (*abhimatā*) F.

अभिमित्र (*abhimitra*) M. "a superior friend", one of the *maruts* (VāP). **अभिमित्रा** (*abhimitrā*) F.

अभियु (*abhiyu*) MF. "one who marches or goes [swiftly]", one of the *maruts* (VāP).

अभिवन्द्य (*abhivandya*) M. "worthy of being saluted or praised", Rāma (RS1). **अभिवन्द्या** (*abhivandyā*) F.

अभिवाद्य (*abhivādya*) M. "worthy of being saluted", Śiva (ŚS1).

अभिवाद्या (*abhivādyā*) F.

अभीमा (*abhīmā*) F. "not frightening", Yamunā (YS). **अभीम** (*abhīma*) M.

अभेद्या (*abhedyā*) F. "she who cannot be divided or pierced", Lakṣmī (LS2), Sītā (SS2). **अभेद्य** (*abhedya*) M.

अभ्यर्चि (*abhyarci*) MF. "one whose brilliance extends to all directions", Yamunā (YS).

अमध्य (*amadhya*) M. "without any middle, infinite", Kṛṣṇa (MBh). **अमध्या** (*amadhyā*) F.

अमर्षण (*amarṣaṇa*) M. "passionate, not tolerating [injustice]", a king (BhP). **अमर्षणा** (*amarṣaṇā*) F.

अमावसु (*amāvasu*) MF. "with riches, prosperous", a king (BrP).

अमिताशन (*amitāśana*) M. "consuming infinitely [at the time of *pralaya*]", Viṣṇu (VS1). **अमिताशना** (*amitāśanā*) F.

अमित्रघ्न (*amitraghna*) M. "the slayer of enemies", epithet of Rāma (VR). **अमित्रघ्नी** (*amitraghnī*) F.

अमुख (*amukha*) M. "not consuming or enjoying (*abhoktā*), abstemious", Śiva (ŚS1). **अमुखा** (*amukhā*) F.

अमूर्ता (*amūrtā*) F. "incorporeal, without a [mortal] body (=having a divine form)", Bhavānī (BS). **अमूर्त** (*amūrta*) M.

अमृताङ्ग (*amṛtāṅga*) M. "he whose body is immortal", Śiva (ŚS3). **अमृताङ्गी** (*amṛtāṅgī*) F.

अमृत्यु (*amṛtyu*) MF. "without death, immortal", Viṣṇu (VS1), Rāma (RS1), Hanumān (HS), Sītā (SS2).

अमेयात्मा (*ameyātmā*) M. "with an immeasurable intellect or mind", Viṣṇu (VS1), Sūrya (SS1), Kṛṣṇa (KS1).

अमोघाक्षी (*amoghākṣī*) F. "she whose eyes (=vision) are unerring or unfailing", a *devī* (MaP). **अमोघाक्ष** (*amoghākṣa*) M.

अम्बुजाक्ष (*ambujākṣa*) M. "lotus-eyed", Kṛṣṇa (KS2). **अम्बुजाक्षी** (*ambujākṣī*) F.

अयस्य (*ayasya*) M. "not to be killed, he who cannot be killed", a *ṛṣi* (VāP). **अयस्या** (*ayasyā*) F.

अयास्य (*ayāsya*) M. "not to be troubled, indefatigable", used for Indra (ṚVŚ), a *ṛṣi* (BhP). **अयास्या** (*ayāsyā*) F.

अयुताक्षरी (*ayutākṣarī*) F. "having tens of thousands of syllables", Sītā (SS2). **अयुताक्षर** (*ayutākṣara*) M.

अयुतायुस् (*ayutāyus*) MF. "one whose age is 10,000 years, he who (=whose name or actions) live forever", a king (BhP).

अयुद्धा (*ayuddhā*) F. "unconquered, invincible", Lakṣmī (LS3). **अयुद्ध** (*ayuddha*) M.

अयोनिज (*ayonija*) M. "not born from a womb, self-born", Viṣṇu (VS1), Sūrya (SS1). **अयोनिजा** (*ayonijā*) F. Annapūrṇā (AS), Durgā (DS3).

अरजा (*arajā*) F. "without dust or impurities, pure", Bhavānī (BS). **अरज** (*araja*) M.

अरविन्दाक्ष (*aravindākṣa*) M. "lotus-eyed", Viṣṇu (MBh). **अरविन्दाक्षी** (*aravindākṣī*) F.

अरागा (*arāgā*) F. "without attachment, dispassionate", Bhavānī (BS). **अराग** (*arāga*) M.

अरिमेजय (*arimejaya*) M. "he who makes his enemies tremble", a king (MBh, VāP). **अरिमेजया** (*arimejayā*) F.

अरिष्टनेमि (*ariṣṭanemi*) M. "with an unhurt felly", an ancestor of Rāma (VR).

अरिष्टा (*ariṣṭā*) F. "unhurt, uninjured, perfect, safe", wife of Kaśyapa who was the mother of Gandharvas (BhP). **अरिष्ट** (*ariṣṭa*) M.

अरोगा (*arogā*) F. "free from [physical and mental] illnesses", a *devī* at Vaidyanātha (MaP). **अरोग** (*aroga*) M.

अरोध्य (*arodhya*) M. "unstoppable, unobstructed, unhindered", Viṣṇu (VS2). **अरोध्या** (*arodhyā*) F.

अरौद्र (*araudra*) M. "not terrifying or fierce, pleasant", Viṣṇu (VS1). **अरौद्री** (*araudrī*) F.

अर्कज (*arkaja*) M. "the son of *arka* (Sūrya)", Śanaiścara (MaP) and also any of Yama, Aśvinīkumāras, Sugrīva, or Karṇa (VK1). **अर्कजा** (*arkajā*) F. Yamunā is the daughter of Sūrya (VāP, BrP).

अर्किणी (*arkiṇī*) F. "bright, radiant, praising, praised", used for Uṣas (ṚVŚ). **अर्की** (*arkī*) M.

अर्चिष्मती (*arciṣmatī*) F. "brilliant, resplendent", Lakṣmī (LS2), daughter of Aṅgiras and Subhā (MBh). **अर्चिष्मान्** (*arciṣmān*) M. Viṣṇu (VS1).

अर्चिसन (*arcisana*) M. "the tree of rays of light, presenting or offering light", a *ṛṣi* (VāP). **अर्चिसना** (*arcisanā*) F.

अर्च्या (*arcyā*) F. "worthy of respect, worship", Yamunā (YS). **अर्च्य** (*arcya*) M.

अर्थद (*arthada*) M. "bestower of wealth or entities", Kṛṣṇa (KS1). **अर्थदा** (*arthadā*) F.

अर्थितव्य (*arthitavya*) M. "desirable, worth asking for", Śiva (ŚS3). **अर्थितव्या** (*arthitavyā*) F.

अर्वावसु (*arvāvasu*) MF. "one whose wealth is near", a *ṛṣi* (MBh).

अर्हन्ती (*arhantī*) F. "she who deserves [something praiseworthy]". **अर्हन्** (*arhan*) M. used for Agni (ṚVŚ).

अलङ्करिष्णु (*alaṅkariṣṇu*) MF. "having ornaments", Rāma (RS1).

अलङ्घ्य (*alaṅghya*) M. "he who cannot be transgressed or passed", Viṣṇu (VS2). **अलङ्घ्या** (*alaṅghyā*) F.

अवदाता (*avadātā*) F. "beautiful, clear, bright, virtuous", Lakṣmī (LS2). **अवदात** (*avadāta*) M.

अवरा (*avarā*) F. "younger, most excellent", Annapūrṇā (AS). **अवर** (*avara*) M.

अवश्या (*avaśyā*) F. "she who cannot be controlled or governed", Lakṣmī (LS3). **अवश्य** (*avaśya*) M.

अवस्यु (*avasyu*) MF. "desirous of protecting, seeking *avana* (love, satisfaction, knowledge, etc.)", epithet of Indra (ṚVŚ).

अविक्षित् (*avikṣit*) MF. "unhurt, unharmed, unimpaired", a king (BhP).

अवित्री (*avitrī*) F. "she who protects", used for the goddesses *div* and *pṛthivī* (ṚVŚ). **अविता** (*avitā*) M.

अविद्ध (*aviddha*) M. "unpierced [in battle], unimpaired, unequalled", a king (VāP). **अविद्धा** (*aviddhā*) F.

अविमुक्ता (*avimuktā*) F. "not free from or bereft of [Śivā]", Durgā (DS3). **अविमुक्त** (*avimukta*) M.

अवेध्या (*avedhyā*) F. "she who cannot be pierced", Yamunā (YS). **अवेध्य** (*avedhya*) M.

अवैरा (*avairā*) F. "free form opposition, enmity, or hostility". **अवैर** (*avaira*) M.

अव्यक्त (*avyakta*) M. "he who cannot be expressed [in words]", Viṣṇu (VS1), Śiva (ŚS1), Rāma (RS1), Kṛṣṇa (KS1), Hanumān (HS). **अव्यक्ता** (*avyaktā*) F. Gāyatrī (GS4), Annapūrṇā (AS).

अव्यग्र (*avyagra*) M. "steady, not agitated or enraged", Hanumān (HS). **अव्यग्रा** (*avyagrā*) F.

अव्यङ्ग (*avyaṅga*) M. "perfect, complete, not defective", Viṣṇu (VS1). **अव्यङ्गा** (*avyaṅgā*) F.

अशून्या (*aśūnyā*) F. "not empty or lacking", Bhavānī (BS). **अशून्य** (*aśūnya*) M.

असिताङ्ग (*asitāṅga*) M. "having a dark body (=complexion)", a *bhairava* (BrP). **असिताङ्गी** (*asitāṅgī*) F.

असुदा (*asudā*) F. "giver of *prāṇas* or life", Gaṅgā (GS3). **असुद** (*asuda*) M.

अहश्चर (*ahaścara*) M. "he who wanders in the day", Śiva (ŚS1). **अहश्चरी** (*ahaścarī*) F.

अहस्कर (*ahaskara*) M. "he who makes (=brings about) the day", Sūrya (AK).

अहिंस्त्र (*ahiṃsra*) M. "harmless, innocent, non-violent", Viṣṇu (VS2). **अहिंस्त्रा** (*ahiṃsrā*) F.

अहिमान् (*ahimān*) M. "having Rāhu [as an opponent]", Sūrya (SS1).

अहिर्बुध्न्य (*ahirbudhnya*) M. "the snake situated at the bottom [of the earth], i.e. Śeṣa", Śiva (ŚS1).

आकर्षिणी (*ākarṣiṇī*) F. "she whose nature is to attract completely, attractive", a *devī* (BrP). **आकर्षी** (*ākarṣī*) M.

आकूति (*ākūti*) F. "intention, wish, she who sounds (=speaks) well", mother of the Yajña incarnation (BhP).

आखुरथ (*ākhuratha*) M. "having a mouse as his chariot", Gaṇeśa (HK).

आखुवाहन (*ākhuvāhana*) M. "having a mouse as his vehicle or mount", Gaṇeśa (BrP).

आग्नीध्र (*āgnīdhra*) M. "he who maintains the Agni", a king (BhP). **आग्नीध्री** (*āgnīdhrī*) F.

आग्नेयी (*āgneyī*) F. "associated with Agni", Gāyatrī (GS4). **आग्नेय** (*āgneya*) M.

आङ्गिरसी (*āṅgirasī*) F. "descendant of Aṅgiras", mother of Viśvakarman (BhP). **आङ्गिरस** (*āṅgirasa*) M.

आज्य (*ājya*) M. "possessing ghee (Agni or a *deva*)", son of Sāvarṇa Manu (VāP). **आज्या** (*ājyā*) F.

आज्यपा (*ājyapā*) F. "she who drinks or protects ghee", Lakṣmī (LS2). **आज्यप** (*ājyapa*) M.

आत्मभू (*ātmabhū*) MF. "existing in the *ātman* (=mind)", Śiva (ŚS3).

आत्मवान् (*ātmavān*) M. "with a controlled mind, patient, prudent", Viṣṇu (VS1), Rāma (RS1), Kṛṣṇa (KS1). **आत्मवती** (*ātmavatī*) F.

आत्मायु (*ātmāyu*) MF. "seeking the *ātman*", a *ṛṣi* (MaP).

आदिकर (*ādikara*) M. "the first creator", Viṣṇu (MBh), Śiva (ŚS1). **आदिकरी** (*ādikarī*) F.

आदिकर्ता (*ādikartā*) M. "the first creator", Rāma (RS1), Viṣṇu (VS2). **आदिकर्त्री** (*ādikartrī*) F.

आदिकेशव (*ādikeśava*) M. "the first one with beautiful hair", Viṣṇu (BrP). **आदिकेशवा** (*ādikeśavā*) F.

आदिजा (*ādijā*) F. "first-born, primeval", Yamunā (YS). **आदिज** (*ādija*) M.

आदिदेव (*ādideva*) M. "the original *deva*, the first god", Viṣṇu (VS2), Rāma (RS1), Dattātreya (DS2). **आदिदेवी** (*ādidevī*) F.

आदिपाल (*ādipāla*) M. "the original nourisher or protector", Viṣṇu (VāP). **आदिपाला** (*ādipālā*) F.

आनक (*ānaka*) M. "he who arouses or energizes", a king (BhP). **आनिका** (*ānikā*) F.

आनर्त (*ānarta*) M. "he who has (=likes) battles, i.e. a warrior or a fighter", a king (BhP). **आनर्ता** (*ānartā*) F.

आपव (*āpava*) M. "the son of Āpu (=Varuṇa)", a *ṛṣi* in the tenth *manvantara* (BrP). **आपवी** (*āpavī*) F.

आप्नुवान् (*āpnuvān*) M. "he who obtains [everything]", a *ṛṣi* (MaP).

आप्य (*āpya*) M. "worth obtaining or knowing", disciple of Yājñavalkya (VāP). **आप्या** (*āpyā*) F.

आप्रवान (*āpravāna*) M. "eager to obtain (*āpra*) and intelligent (*vāna*)", a *ṛṣi* (BrP).

आमुक्त (*āmukta*) M. "completely liberated", Sūrya (SS1). **आमुक्ता** (*āmuktā*) F.

आमोदिनी (*āmodinī*) F. "fragrant, happy, delighted", Rādhā (RKS). **आमोदी** (*āmodī*) M.

आयति (*āyati*) MF. "one who reaches (=knows) completely", son of Nahuṣa (BhP), daughter of Meru (BhP).

आयाप्य (*āyāpya*) M. "worth obtaining (=knowing) completely", a *ṛṣi* (VāP). **आयाप्या** (*āyāpyā*) F.

आयुर्दा (*āyurdā*) F. "she who gives life", a river (BhP). **आयुर्द** (*āyurda*) M.

आरब्ध (*ārabdha*) M. "he who has commenced", a king (BhP). **आरब्धा** (*ārabdhā*) F.

आरित (*ārita*) M. "he who is praised, he who is situated in *stomas*", used for Indra (ṚVŚ). **आरिता** (*āritā*) F.

आर्यव (*āryava*) M. "he whose behaviour is honourable", a *ṛṣi* (VāP). **आर्यवा** (*āryavā*) F.

आलम्बी (*ālambī*) M. "he whose nature is to support or maintain [others]", a *ṛṣi* (BrP). **आलम्बिनी** (*ālambinī*) F.

आलोकित (*ālokita*) M. "one who is (or who has been) seen or beheld". **आलोकिता** (*ālokitā*) F.

आलोक्य (*ālokya*) M. "worth seeing". **आलोक्या** (*ālokyā*) F.

आवन्त्य (*āvantya*) M. "belonging to Avantī (Ujjain)", a *ṛṣi* (BhP). **आवन्ती** (*āvantī*) F.

आवर्तन (*āvartana*) M. "he who turns around [the wheel of time]", Viṣṇu (VS1). **आवर्तना** (*āvartanā*) F. Gāyatrī (GS4).

आवर्तिनी (*āvartinī*) F. "turning around, having whirlpools", Yamunā (YS). **आवर्ती** (*āvartī*) M.

आविर्होत्र (*āvirhotra*) M. "he whose offerings [in a *yajña*] are evident", a *ṛṣi* (BhP). **आविर्होत्रा** (*āvirhotrā*) F.

आवेद (*āveda*) M. "he whose knowledge is all-round (=complete)", a *ṛṣi* (MaP). **आवेदा** (*āvedā*) F.

आवेद्य (*āvedya*) M. "he who is worth knowing entirely, he who can be [only] partially known", Śiva (ŚS5). **आवेद्या** (*āvedyā*) F.

आशुग (*āśuga*) M. "moving quickly, swift", Sūrya (SS1). **आशुगा** (*āśugā*) F.

आस्तिकी (*āstikī*) F. "she who believes [in Vedas], pious, faithful". **आस्तिक** (*āstika*) M.

आहार्य (*āhārya*) M. "to be worshipped", a *ṛṣi* (VāP). **आहार्या** (*āhāryā*) F.

आहुक (*āhuka*) M. "he who performs *yajñas*", a king (BhP). **आहुकी** (*āhukī*) F. a queen who was the sister of Āhuka (BhP).

इन्द्रद्युम्न (*indradyumna*) M. "having the *dyumnas* (glories, powers, opulences, etc.) of Indra", a king (BhP). **इन्द्रद्युम्ना** (*indradyumnā*) F.

इन्द्रानुज (*indrānuja*) M. "younger brother of Indra", Narasiṃha (NS), Viṣṇu (MBh).

इन्द्रार्चित (*indrārcita*) M. "revered by Indra", Kṛṣṇa (RKS). **इन्द्रार्चिता** (*indrārcitā*) F.

इन्द्रोत (*indrota*) M. "protected by Indra", a *ṛṣi* (BrP). **इन्द्रोता**

(*indrotā*) F.

इरावती (*irāvatī*) F. "with praiseworthy speech, possessing *irā* (earth, speech, or water)", Gāyatrī (GS4), Gaṅgā (GS3). **इरावान्** (*irāvān*) M. son of Arjuna (MBh).

इषिर (*iṣira*) M. "he who moves [quickly], strong, vigorous, active, quick", used for Vāyu (ṚVŚ). **इषिरा** (*iṣirā*) F.

इषुमान् (*iṣumān*) M. "having many or praiseworthy arrows, an archer", a king (BhP). **इषुमती** (*iṣumatī*) F.

इष्टदा (*iṣṭadā*) F. "giving what is desired", Gāyatrī (GS4). **इष्टद** (*iṣṭada*) M.

ईलिन (*īlina*) M. "he who is worshipped", a king (MBh). **ईलिनी** (*īlinī*) F. a princess (HV).

ईशित्री (*īśitrī*) F. "she who rules or governs", Lalitā (LTS). **ईशिता** (*īśitā*) M.

उक्षा (*ukṣā*) F. "she who cleanses [*pāpas*]", Gaṅgā (GS3). **उक्ष** (*ukṣa*) M.

उग्रतपस् (*ugratapas*) MF. "one whose *tapas* (askesis) is fierce or strong", a *ṛṣi* (VāP).

उग्ररेतस् (*ugraretas*) M. "he whose seed (=son, i.e. Skanda) is unbearable (=invincible)", Rudra/Śiva (BhP).

उग्रायुध (*ugrāyudha*) M. "he whose weapons are strong or formidable", a king (BhP). **उग्रायुधा** (*ugrāyudhā*) F.

उग्रेश (*ugreśa*) M. "the lord of the mighty or fierce", Viṣṇu

(VS2), Śiva (MBh). **उग्रेशी** (*ugreśī*) F.

उडुपति (*uḍupati*) M. "the lord of the constellations or stars", Candra or the moon (ViP).

उडुराट् (*uḍurāṭ*) M. "lord of the stars", Candra or the moon (ViP).

उत्कला (*utkalā*) F. "skilled in the arts, she whose arts are excellent", a queen (BhP). **उत्कल** (*utkala*) M.

उत्कृष्टा (*utkṛṣṭā*) F. "excellent, eminent, the best", mother of *autkārṣṭeya rākṣasas* (BrP). **उत्कृष्ट** (*utkṛṣṭa*) M.

उत्तारक (*uttāraka*) M. "he who enables [devotees] to cross over [the ocean of transmigration]", Śiva (ŚS3). **उत्तारिका** (*uttārikā*) F.

उत्पलाक्षी (*utpalākṣī*) F. "she whose eyes are beautiful like the blue lotus", a *devī* (MaP). **उत्पलाक्ष** (*utpalākṣa*) M.

उत्सङ्ग (*utsaṅga*) M. "solitary", Śiva (ŚS1). **उत्सङ्गा** (*utsaṅgā*) F.

उत्सर्ग (*utsarga*) M. "he whose creations are excellent", son of Mitra (BhP). **उत्सर्गा** (*utsargā*) F.

उत्सुका (*utsukā*) F. "eager, striving, zealous, fond of", Sītā (SS2), Gomātā (GS6). **उत्सुक** (*utsuka*) M. son of Balarāma (VāP).

उदक्या (*udakyā*) F. "existing in waters", Bhavānī (BS). **उदक्य** (*udakya*) M.

उदग्र (*udagra*) M. "lofty, noble", Śiva (ŚS1). **उदग्रा** (*udagrā*) F.

उदर्षि (*udarṣi*) M. "an excellent seer (*ṛṣi*)", son of Devakī (BrP).

उदीची (*udīcī*) F. "she who moves upwards (or north)", a river (VāP). **उदङ्** (*udaṅ*) M.

उद्गाता (*udgātā*) M. "an excellent singer, he who sings aloud", the reciter of *sāmans* (AK), Sūrya (SS1). **उद्गात्री** (*udgātrī*) F.

उद्गीथ (*udgītha*) M. "he whose song or speech is excellent", a king (BhP). **उद्गीथा** (*udgīthā*) F.

उद्भवा (*udbhavā*) F. "she whose existence is eminent", Lakṣmī (LS2). **उद्भव** (*udbhava*) M.

उद्यमा (*udyamā*) F. "she whose *yama* (self-control) is excellent", Durgā (DS3). **उद्यम** (*udyama*) M.

उद्रीति (*udrīti*) MF. "one who has an excellent disposition", Lakṣmī (LS2).

उन्नेता (*unnetā*) M. "an excellent leader, he who leads upwards", one of the sixteen *ṛtviks* (MaP). **उन्नेत्री** (*unnetrī*) F.

उन्माद (*unmada*) M. "infatuating, causing passion", Śiva (ŚS1).

उपदेव (*upadeva*) M. "a minor or young *deva*", a king (BhP). **उपदेवी** (*upadevī*) F. wife of Vasudeva (MaP).

उपदेवा (*upadevā*) F. "she who shines nearby (when in proximity)", a princess (BhP).

उपशान्त (*upaśānta*) M. "calm, peaceful, tranquil", Śiva (ŚS1). **उपशान्ता** (*upaśāntā*) F.

उपश्लोक (*upaśloka*) M. "close to (=fond of) *ślokas*", father of Brahmasāvarṇi Manu (BhP). **उपश्लोका** (*upaślokā*) F.

उमाधव (*umādhava*) M. "the husband of Umā (Pārvatī)", Śiva (ŚS1).

उरगेश (*urageśa*) M. "lord of serpents (Śeṣa)", similar to the epithet *urageśvara* mentioned in ViP. **उरगेशी** (*urageśī*) F.

उरुक्रम (*urukrama*) M. "having large strides [as Vāmana]", Viṣṇu (MBh, VS2), Kṛṣṇa (KS1). **उरुक्रमा** (*urukramā*) F.

उरुक्रिय (*urukriya*) M. "he whose acts are great", a king (BhP). **उरुक्रिया** (*urukriyā*) F.

उरुगाय (*urugāya*) M. "sung (=praised) by the great", Kṛṣṇa/ Viṣṇu (BhP). **उरुगाया** (*urugāyā*) F.

उरुगीत (*urugīta*) M. "much sung (=praised)", Kṛṣṇa (KS1). **उरुगीता** (*urugītā*) F.

उरुश्रवस् (*uruśravas*) MF. "one whose fame is great (far-reaching)", a king (BhP).

उल्लसन्ती (*ullasantī*) F. "sparkling, brilliant, rising, sportive", Yamunā (YS). **उल्लसन्** (*ullasan*) M.

उशद्रथ (*uśadratha*) M. "he whose chariot is beautiful", a king (BrP). **उशद्रथा** (*uśadrathā*) F.

उशिक (*uśika*) M. "he who shines or is brilliant", a king (BhP). **उशिका** (*uśikā*) F.

उशिज (*uśija*) M. "eager, zealous, desirous", a *ṛṣi* (BrP). **उशिजा**

(*uśijā*) F.

उशीनर (*uśīnara*) M. "he who fulfils wishes", a king (BhP).

उषङ्गु (*uṣaṅgu*) MF. "with burning (fiercely brilliant) rays", Śiva (ŚS1).

उषित (*uṣita*) M. "quick, swift", a *deva* (VāP). **उषिता** (*uṣitā*) F.

उष्णिक् (*uṣṇik*) F. "loving eminently", Yamunā (YS), a Vedic metre and a horse of Sūrya (BhP).

ऊर्जवह (*ūrjavaha*) M. "bearer of strength, strong", a king (ViP). **ऊर्जवहा** (*ūrjavahā*) F.

ऊर्जश्री (*ūrjaśrī*) F. "she whose *śrī* (affluence, prosperity, abundance, opulence, brilliance, fame, growth, success, etc.) is strong", a queen (BrP).

ऊर्जस्वान् (*ūrjasvān*) M. "powerful, strong", Hanumān (HS), Gaṇeśa (GS2). **ऊर्जस्वती** (*ūrjasvatī*) F. Durgā (DS3), wife of Śukra (BhP).

ऊर्जस्वी (*ūrjasvī*) M. "strong, powerful, mighty", son of Bhautya Manu (BrP). **ऊर्जस्विनी** (*ūrjasvinī*) F.

ऊर्जावती (*ūrjāvatī*) F. "possessing power or strength", Gaṅgā (GS3). **ऊर्जावान्** (*ūrjāvān*) M.

ऊर्ध्वगा (*ūrdhvagā*) F. "ascending, high", Yamunā (YS). **ऊर्ध्वग** (*ūrdhvaga*) M.

ऊर्ध्वा (*ūrdhvā*) F. "upright, elevated, superior", Gāyatrī (GS4). **ऊर्ध्व** (*ūrdhva*) M.

ऋग्मिय (*ṛgmiya*) M. "praiseworthy, approaching the *ṛcs*", used for Indra (ṚVŚ). **ऋग्मिया** (*ṛgmiyā*) F.

ऋग्मी (*ṛgmī*) M. "praiseworthy", used for Indra (ṚVŚ). **ऋग्मिनी** (*ṛgminī*) F.

ऋग्वेदा (*ṛgvedā*) F. "having the form of Ṛgveda", Gāyatrī (GS4).

ऋङ्मय (*ṛṅmaya*) M. "consisting of mantras of Ṛgveda, he whose form (*svarūpa*) is the Ṛgveda", Śiva (ŚS4). **ऋङ्मयी** (*ṛṅmayī*) F. Durgā (a sahasranāma from an unknown source).

ऋचीक (*ṛcīka*) M. "knowing *ṛcs* (mantras of Ṛgveda)", father of Jamadagni (BrP).

ऋचेयु (*ṛceyu*) MF. "seeking *ṛcs* (mantras of Ṛgveda)", a king (MBh).

ऋजिष्ठ (*ṛjiṣṭha*) M. "most honest, most straightforward", example cited in Kāś. **ऋजिष्ठा** (*ṛjiṣṭhā*) F.

ऋजीयान् (*ṛjīyān*) M. "more (=most) honest or straightforward", neuter form (*ṛjīyas*) used for truthfulness (ṚVŚ). **ऋजीयसी** (*ṛjīyasī*) F.

ऋजीष (*ṛjīṣa*) M. "he who throws away [enemies]", Indra (ṚVŚ). **ऋजीषा** (*ṛjīṣā*) F.

ऋजुगा (*ṛjugā*) F. "she who goes by the straight path or the honest way", used for divine speech (KYT). **ऋजुग** (*ṛjuga*) M.

ऋजुदाय (*ṛjudāya*) M. "he whose gifts are beneficial", son of

Devakī (BrP).

ऋज्वी (*ṛjvī*) F. "straight, right, honest, favourable", Gāyatrī (GS4). **ऋजु** (*ṛju*) M.

ऋणवान् (*ṛṇavān*) M. "indebted, having (=acknowledging) the [three] debts", a *ṛṣi* (MaP). **ऋणवती** (*ṛṇavatī*) F.

ऋतजित् (*ṛtajit*) MF. "conqueror of *ṛta* (truth)", a Yakṣa (ViP).

ऋतज्य (*ṛtajya*) M. "he whose bowstring is truth [alone]", used for the bow of Brahmaṇaspati (ṚVŚ). **ऋतज्या** (*ṛtajyā*) F.

ऋतञ्जय (*ṛtañjaya*) M. "conqueror of *ṛta* (truth)", Vyāsa in eighteenth *Dvāpara* (VāP). **ऋतञ्जया** (*ṛtañjayā*) F.

ऋतद्युम्न (*ṛtadyumna*) M. "resplendent due to truth", used for Soma (ṚVŚ). **ऋतद्युम्ना** (*ṛtadyumnā*) F.

ऋतधामा (*ṛtadhāmā*) M. "the abode of truth", Indra of twelfth *manvantara* (BhP).

ऋतध्वज (*ṛtadhvaja*) M. "he who has the flag of truth, truthful", Rudra/Śiva (BhP). **ऋतध्वजा** (*ṛtadhvajā*) F.

ऋतपा (*ṛtapā*) F. "she who protects or guards truth", Uṣas (ṚVŚ). **ऋतप** (*ṛtapa*) M.

ऋतयु (*ṛtayu*) MF. "seeking truth or *yajña*", used for Indra (ṚVŚ).

ऋतवाक (*ṛtavāka*) M. "he whose speech is truthful", a *ṛṣi* (BrP). **ऋतवाका** (*ṛtavākā*) F.

ऋतश्री (*ṛtaśrī*) MF. "having the *śrī* (brilliance) of truth, resting on truth", used for Vedī (KYT).

ऋतसेन (*ṛtasena*) M. "he whose army (=power) is truth", a *gandharva* (BhP). **ऋतसेना** (*ṛtasenā*) F.

ऋतस्तुप् (*ṛtastup*) MF. "speaking the truth", a *ṛṣi* (ṚVŚ).

ऋतस्था (*ṛtasthā*) F. "standing right, situated in truth". **ऋतस्थ** (*ṛtastha*) M.

ऋतस्पति (*ṛtaspati*) M. "the lord of *yajñas*, the protector of truth", used for Vāyu (ṚVŚ, ŚYM).

ऋतुकर (*ṛtukara*) M. "he who causes the seasons [at the right time]", Śiva (ŚS5). **ऋतुकरी** (*ṛtukarī*) F.

ऋतुध्वज (*ṛtudhvaja*) M. "he whose banner is light or brilliance", Narasiṃha (NS). **ऋतुध्वजा** (*ṛtudhvajā*) F.

ऋतुमती (*ṛtumatī*) F. "enjoying the seasons, a young girl", Gāyatrī (GS4). **ऋतुमान्** (*ṛtumān*) M.

ऋतेयु (*ṛteyu*) MF. "wishing for truth", a king (BhP).

ऋद्धिता (*ṛddhitā*) F. "made to increase of prosper". **ऋद्धित** (*ṛddhita*) M.

ऋद्धिदा (*ṛddhidā*) F. "bestower of *ṛddhi* (growth, success, prosperity)", Gāyatrī (GS4). **ऋद्धिद** (*ṛddhida*) M.

ऋभवा (*ṛbhavā*) F. "originating from Aditi (the mother of the *devas*)", Annapūrṇā (AS). **ऋभव** (*ṛbhava*) M.

ऋषिक (*ṛṣika*) M. "a minor or young *ṛṣi*", a king (MBh), son of a *ṛṣi* (BrP). **ऋषिका** (*ṛṣikā*) F.

ऋषिज (*ṛṣija*) M. "born from a *ṛṣi*", a *ṛṣi* (MaP). **ऋषिजा** (*ṛṣijā*) F.

एकवीरा (*ekavīrā*) F. "the only brave or heroic one, the bravest", Lakṣmī (LS2), Annapūrṇā (AS). **एकवीर** (*ekavīra*) M.

एकाक्ष (*ekākṣa*) M. "having only one means of knowledge (=knowledge itself)", Śiva (LiP). **एकाक्षा** (*ekākṣā*) F.

एकाङ्गी (*ekāṅgī*) F. "having a unique body or form", Rādhā (RS2). **एकाङ्ग** (*ekāṅga*) M.

एकात्मा (*ekātmā*) M. "the one *ātman*, the main *ātman*", Kṛṣṇa (KS1).

एकायन (*ekāyana*) M. "having only one recourse, attentive, intent", a *ṛṣi* (MaP). **एकायना** (*ekāyanā*) F.

ऐक्ष्वाक (*aikṣvāka*) M. "a descendant of Ikṣvāku", Rāma (VR). **ऐक्ष्वाकी** (*aikṣvākī*) F. a queen (MaP).

ऐतिह्या (*aitihyā*) F. "traditional, legendary", Gaṅgā (GS3). **ऐतिह्य** (*aitihya*) M.

ऐन्दवी (*aindavī*) F. "associated with the moon", Lakṣmī (LS2). **ऐन्दव** (*aindava*) M.

ऐन्द्री (*aindrī*) F. "belonging to Indra, associated with Indra, the energy of Indra", Bhavānī (BS), Lakṣmī (LS2), Sītā (SS2), Gāyatrī (GS4). **ऐन्द्र** (*aindra*) M. Arjuna, the son of Indra (ŚK,

VK1).

ऐश्वर्यदा (*aiśvaryadā*) F. “bestower of power, supremacy, or affluence”, Gaṅgā (GS3). **ऐश्वर्यद** (*aiśvaryada*) M.

ओघवती (*oghavatī*) F. “with [many] streams, possessing abundance [of virtues]”, a queen (BhP). **ओघवान्** (*oghavān*) M. a king (MBh, BhP).

ओजस्कर (*ojaskara*) M. “the cause of strength, giving strength”, Śiva (ŚS3). **ओजस्करी** (*ojaskarī*) F.

ओजस्वान् (*ojasvān*) M. “possessing power or splendour”, Gaṇeśa (GS2). **ओजस्वती** (*ojasvatī*) F.

ओजस्विनी (*ojasvinī*) F. “brilliant, powerful”, Gaṅgā (GS3). **ओजस्वी** (*ojasvī*) M.

ओजिष्ठ (*ojiṣṭha*) M. “strongest, mightiest, most powerful”, a *deva* (MaP). **ओजिष्ठा** (*ojiṣṭhā*) F.

ओजोदा (*ojodā*) F. “she who gives brilliance or power”, Gaṅgā (GS3). **ओजोद** (*ojoda*) M.

ओजोवती (*ojovatī*) F. “possessing power or brilliance”, Lalitā (LS1). **ओजोवान्** (*ojovān*) M.

ओता (*otā*) F. “interwoven [with the world], extending (=pervading the universe)”, Gāyatrī (GS4). **ओत** (*ota*) M.

ओषधीश (*oṣadhīśa*) M. “lord of the herbs”, Candra or the moon (MaP).

औक्षि (*aukṣi*) M. “son of Ukṣa”, a king (MaP). **औक्षी** (*aukṣī*) F.

औग्री (*augrī*) F. "associated with Ugra (Śiva)", Gaṅgā (GS3). **औग्र** (*augra*) M.

औत्तम (*auttama*) M. "son of Uttama, associated with the best", the third Manu (MaP). **औत्तमी** (*auttamī*) F.

औदार्य (*audārya*) M. "possessing generosity or magnanimity", son of Aṅgiras (VāP).

औपगव (*aupagava*) M. "descendant of Upagu (=he who is close to the cows)", a *ṛṣi* (MaP). **औपगवी** (*aupagavī*) F. cited in PMB.

औपेन्द्री (*aupendrī*) F. "associated with Upendra (Viṣṇu)", Gaṅgā (GS3). **औपेन्द्र** (*aupendra*) M.

और्व (*aurva*) M. "born from the thigh (*ūru*), son of or related to the earth (*urvī*)", a *ṛṣi* (MBh). **और्वी** (*aurvī*) F.

और्वशेय (*aurvaśeya*) M. "born from (=due to Urvaśī)", Agastya and Vasiṣṭha (as per BD). **और्वशेयी** (*aurvaśeyī*) F.

और्वा (*aurvā*) F. "found in (=pervading) the earth", Gāyatrī (GS4).

औशिज (*auśija*) M. "eager, zealous, desirous", a *ṛṣi* (VāP). **औशिजी** (*auśijī*) F.

कंसारि (*kaṃsāri*) M. "enemy of Kaṃsa", Viṣṇu (VS2), Kṛṣṇa (RKS).

कक्षेयु (*kakṣeyu*) MF. "desiring the interiors of forests (=solitude)", a king (MaP, VāP).

कञ्जस्था (*kañjasthā*) F. "situated in the lotus", Annapūrṇā (AS). **कञ्जस्थ** (*kañjastha*) M.

कञ्जाक्षी (*kañjākṣī*) F. "lotus-eyed", Sarasvatī (SS3). **कञ्जाक्ष** (*kañjākṣa*) M.

कञ्जाभा (*kañjābhā*) F. "having the splendour or beauty of a lotus", Annapūrṇā (AS). **कञ्जाभ** (*kañjābha*) M.

कण्व (*kaṇva*) M. "intelligent, he who praises, worthy of being praised", a king (BhP), a *ṛṣi* (BhP). **कण्वा** (*kaṇvā*) F.

कथक (*kathaka*) M. "he who speaks or narrates, an actor/performer", Gaṇeśa (GS2). **कथिका** (*kathikā*) F.

कथित (*kathita*) M. "expressed [by Vedas], celebrated, extolled", Viṣṇu (VS1). **कथिता** (*kathitā*) F.

कथ्य (*kathya*) M. "he who should be spoken about, notable", Śiva (ŚS4). **कथ्या** (*kathyā*) F.

कदम्बेशी (*kadambeśī*) F. "the goddess of fragrance", Lalitā (BrP). **कदम्बेश** (*kadambeśa*) M.

कन्यका (*kanyakā*) F. "a young girl", Yogamāyā (BhP).

कपर्दिनी (*kapardinī*) F. "possessing braided hair, wife of Kapardī (=Śiva)", Annapūrṇā (AS), Lalitā (LS1). **कपर्दी** (*kapardī*) M.

कपर्दीश (*kapardīśa*) M. "the ruler who has matted hair, the lord of those with matted hair (=ascetics)", Śiva (VāP).

कपिञ्जल (*kapiñjala*) M. "he who moves [swiftly] like a *kapi*, he who speaks mellifluously", a *ṛṣi* (MaP). **कपिञ्जली** (*kapiñjalī*) F. wife of Vasiṣṭha (BrP).

कपिध्वज (*kapidhvaja*) M. "he whose flag has [the mark of] *kapi* (Hanumān)", Arjuna (AK, BG).

कमलाभ (*kamalābha*) M. "having the splendour or beauty of a lotus", Kṛṣṇa (KS2). **कमलाभा** (*kamalābhā*) F.

कम्प्रा (*kamprā*) F. "quick, agile, swift", Gāyatrī (GS4). **कम्प्र** (*kampra*) M.

कर्मजित् (*karmajit*) MF. "one who has conquered *karma* (= destiny)", a king (BhP).

कर्मदा (*karmadā*) F. "the bestower of actions", Annapūrṇā (AS). **कर्मद** (*karmada*) M.

कर्षिणी (*karṣiṇī*) F. "attractive", Lakṣmī (LS2), Sītā (SS2). **कर्षी** (*karṣī*) M.

कल्पिनी (*kalpinī*) F. "having a good *kalpa* (resolve)", Bhavānī (BS). **कल्पी** (*kalpī*) M.

कव्याग्नि (*kavyāgni*) M. "the Agni for oblations to ancestors", a type of Agni (VāP).

काञ्चनाक्षी (*kāñcanākṣī*) F. "having golden eyes", Gaṅgā (GS3). **काञ्चनाक्ष** (*kāñcanākṣa*) M.

कामघ्न (*kāmaghna*) M. "the slayer of *kāma* (lust)", Dattātreya (DS2). **कामघ्नी** (*kāmaghnī*) F.

कामेशी (*kāmeśī*) F. "the goddess (= bestower) of [all] wishes",

Rādhā (RS2), Lalitā (BrP). **कामेश** (*kāmeśa*) M.

कारुणिक (*kāruṇika*) M. "compassionate", Sūrya (SS1), Rāma (RS1). **कारुणिकी** (*kāruṇikī*) F.

कालघ्न (*kālaghna*) M. "the slayer of time, transcending time", Sūrya (SS1). **कालघ्नी** (*kālaghnī*) F.

कालस्था (*kālasthā*) F. "situated in all times, eternal", Annapūrṇā (AS). **कालस्थ** (*kālastha*) M.

कालात्मा (*kālātmā*) M. "having the nature of *kāla*", Rāma (RS1).

काशिनी (*kāśinī*) F. "she who shines, resplendent". **काशी** (*kāśī*) M. a *brāhmaṇa* who was son of Kavi (MBh).

काशेय (*kāśeya*) M. "belonging to Kāśī (Benares)", a king (BrP). **काशेयी** (*kāśeyī*) F.

काश्या (*kāśyā*) F. "from Kāśī (Benares)", a queen (MBh). **काश्य** (*kāśya*) M. a king (MBh).

कीर्तिता (*kīrtitā*) F. "praised, celebrated", Durgā (DS4). **कीर्तित** (*kīrtita*) M.

कीर्तिदा (*kīrtidā*) F. "she who bestows fame or glory", Sarasvatī (SS3), Durgā (DS3). **कीर्तिद** (*kīrtida*) M. Rāma (RS1), Hanumān (HS).

कीर्तिमती (*kīrtimatī*) F. "famous, celebrated, renowned", a queen (BrP). **कीर्तिमान्** (*kīrtimān*) M.

कीर्तिरथ (*kīrtiratha*) M. "he whose chariot is his [far-spread] fame", a king (BrP).

कीर्त्या (*kīrtyā*) F. "deserving praise, praiseworthy". **कीर्त्य** (*kīrtya*) M.

कीलिनी (*kīlinī*) F. "she who has stakes or pins", the earth (VK2).

कुत्स (*kutsa*) M. "he who condemns or despises [that which is evil]", a *ṛṣi* (ṚVŚ), son of Cākṣuṣa Manu (BhP). **कुत्सा** (*kutsā*) F.

कुधरा (*kudharā*) F. "bearing or supporting the earth", Gāyatrī (GS4). **कुधर** (*kudhara*) M.

कुन्दर (*kundara*) M. "the bestower of [pure fruits like] *kunda*", Viṣṇu (VS1). **कुन्दरा** (*kundarā*) F.

कुमुदाक्ष (*kumudākṣa*) M. "lotus-eyed", attendant of Viṣṇu (BhP). **कुमुदाक्षी** (*kumudākṣī*) F.

कुम्भज (*kumbhaja*) M. "born from the pitcher", Agastya (BrP).

कुलिका (*kulikā*) F. "having a [noble] family", Lakṣmī (LS3). **कुलिक** (*kulika*) M.

कुल्या (*kulyā*) F. "well-born, respectable", Annapūrṇā (AS). **कुल्य** (*kulya*) M.

कुशाम्ब (*kuśāmba*) M. "he who reaches (=obtains) the *kuśa* grass", a king (BhP).

कुशावर्त (*kuśāvarta*) M. "he who revolves (=has in abundance) the *kuśa* grass", son of Ṛṣabha (BhP).

कुशिक (*kuśika*) M. “possessing the *kuśa* grass”, a *ṛṣi* (VāP). **कुशिका** (*kuśikā*) F.

कुशेशय (*kuśeśaya*) M. “sleeping in the water [of *kṣīrasāgara*]”, Narasiṃha (NS). **कुशेशया** (*kuśeśayā*) F.

कृतञ्जय (*kṛtañjaya*) M. “conqueror of destiny”, a king (BhP). **कृतञ्जया** (*kṛtañjayā*) F.

कृतागम (*kṛtāgama*) M. “the origin of [all] creation or actions”, Narasiṃha (NS). **कृतागमा** (*kṛtāgamā*) F.

कृताग्नि (*kṛtāgni*) M. “he who has done (=maintained) the fires”, a king (BhP).

कृतान्त (*kṛtānta*) M. “he who has reached the end (=conclusion)”, son of Svārociṣa Manu (VāP), Yama (MaP). **कृतान्ता** (*kṛtāntā*) F.

कृतावर्त (*kṛtāvarta*) M. “he who makes the creation go round”, Narasiṃha (NS). **कृतावर्ता** (*kṛtāvartā*) F.

कृतिमान् (*kṛtimān*) M. “he whose deeds are praiseworthy”, a king (BhP). **कृतिमती** (*kṛtimatī*) F.

कृतेयु (*kṛteyu*) MF. “desiring work or action”, a king (VāP).

कृत्तिवास (*kṛttivāsa*) M. “clothed in the hide of an elephant”, Śiva (ŚS2).

कृत्वी (*kṛtvī*) F. “causing [welfare]”, a queen (BhP).

कृपावती (*kṛpāvatī*) F. “compassionate”, Bhavānī (BS). **कृपावान्** (*kṛpāvān*) M.

कृपी (*kṛpī*) F. "she who has compassion", wife of Droṇa (MBh). **कृप** (*kṛpa*) M.

कृशोदरी (*kṛśodarī*) F. "having a slender waist", Bhavānī (BS). **कृशोदर** (*kṛśodara*) M.

कृष्णदा (*kṛṣṇadā*) F. "she who gives (= leads to) Kṛṣṇa", Rādhā (RKS).

कृष्णेशी (*kṛṣṇeśī*) F. "the goddess of Kṛṣṇa", Rādhā (RS2). **कृष्णेश** (*kṛṣṇeśa*) M. "lord of Kṛṣṇa, he whose lord is Kṛṣṇa", one of the *liṅgas* (ŚiP).

केतुमान् (*ketumān*) M. "possessing light or brightness", Sūrya (SS1). **केतुमती** (*ketumatī*) F.

केलिमान् (*kelimān*) M. "having many pastimes", Kṛṣṇa (KS1). **केलिमती** (*kelimatī*) F.

केवला (*kevalā*) F. "the only one", Lakṣmī (LS2), Rādhā (RS2). **केवल** (*kevala*) M.

कैशिक (*kaiśika*) M. "possessing [fine] hair", a king (BrP). **कैशिकी** (*kaiśikī*) F.

कोमलिका (*komalikā*) F. "delicate, beautiful, agreeable", Gomātā (GS6). **कोमलक** (*komalaka*) M.

कोविदारी (*kovidārī*) F. "tearing or splitting the earth", a *mātṛkā* (MaP). **कोविदार** (*kovidāra*) M.

कोशदा (*kośadā*) F. "bestower of treasures", Bhavānī (BS). **कोशद** (*kośada*) M.

कोहल (*kohala*) M. "he who ploughs the earth, he who astonishes", a *ṛṣi* (MBh). **कोहला** (*kohalā*) F.

कौत्स (*kautsa*) M. "descendant of Kutsa", a *ṛṣi* (MaP). **कौत्सी** (*kautsī*) F.

कौलिनी (*kaulinī*) F. "worshipped in [every] house or family", Annapūrṇā (AS), Lalitā (LS1). **कौली** (*kaulī*) M.

क्रतु (*kratu*) M. "[being the] *yajña* with *yūpa*", Viṣṇu (VS1).

क्रतुञ्जय (*kratuñjaya*) M. "conqueror of powers", Veda Vyāsa of seventeenth *Dvāpara* (ViP). **क्रतुञ्जया** (*kratuñjayā*) F.

क्रतुमती (*kratumatī*) F. "intelligent, wise, powerful", Gāyatrī (GS4). **क्रतुमान्** (*kratumān*) M. son of Viśvāmitra (BhP).

क्रोधघ्न (*krodhaghna*) M. "the slayer of *krodha* (anger)", Dattātreya (DS2). **क्रोधघ्नी** (*krodhaghnī*) F.

क्षेत्रेशी (*kṣetreśī*) F. "ruler of *kṣetra* (matter or body)", Lalitā (LS1). **क्षेत्रेश** (*kṣetreśa*) M.

क्षेमक (*kṣemaka*) M. "possessing/causing prosperity", a king (BhP). **क्षेमिका** (*kṣemikā*) F.

क्षेमङ्करी (*kṣemaṅkarī*) F. "causing well-being or *kṣema* (protecting what is obtained)", Annapūrṇā (AS). **क्षेमङ्कर** (*kṣemaṅkara*) M.

क्षेमजित् (*kṣemajit*) MF. "conqueror of prosperity", a king (MaP).

क्षेम्य (*kṣemya*) M. "healthy, prosperous, tranquil", a king

(BhP). **क्षेम्या** (*kṣemyā*) F.

खगस्था (*khagasthā*) F. "situated in *khaga* (=the sun)", Annapūrṇā (AS). **खगस्थ** (*khagastha*) M.

खगेशी (*khageśī*) F. "the best among the *khagas* (=deities)", Annapūrṇā (AS). **खगेश** (*khageśa*) M.

खञ्जन (*khañjana*) M. "led by a lame [charioteer] (Aruṇa)", Sūrya (SS1).

खद्योत (*khadyota*) M. "illuminating the sky", Sūrya (SS1). **खद्योता** (*khadyotā*) F.

खनित्र (*khanitra*) M. "he who digs (=uproots) [his opponents]", a king (BhP). **खनित्रा** (*khanitrā*) F.

खस्था (*khasthā*) F. "situated in the sky", Gaṅgā (GS3). **खस्थ** (*khastha*) M.

खेचरी (*khecarī*) F. "moving in the sky", a *mudrā* in Yoga (HYP), Annapūrṇā (AS), Gaṅgā (GS3). **खेचर** (*khecara*) M. a *vidyādhara* or a divine being (BhP).

ख्याता (*khyātā*) F. "famous, well-known, renowned", Gāyatrī (GS4). **ख्यात** (*khyāta*) M.

गणक (*gaṇaka*) M. "he who calculates, a mathematician, an astrologer", Gaṇeśa (GS1).

गणञ्जय (*gaṇañjaya*) M. "the conqueror of *gaṇas*", Gaṇeśa (GS2). **गणञ्जया** (*gaṇañjayā*) F.

गणाधिप (*gaṇādhipa*) M. "the emperor of the *gaṇas*", Gaṇeśa

(GS1). **गणाधिपा** (*gaṇādhipā*) F.

गतामय (*gatāmaya*) M. "whose faults or illnesses have gone", Gaṇeśa (GS1). **गतामया** (*gatāmayā*) F.

गतीश/गतीश्वर (*gatīśa/gatīśvara*) M. "the lord of movements, the best recourse or shelter", *gatīśvara* is a name of Gaṇeśa (GS1). **गतीशी/गतीश्वरी** (*gatīśī/gatīśvarī*) F.

गदाग्रज (*gadāgraja*) M. "born before Gada (younger brother of Vasudeva)", Viṣṇu (VS1), Kṛṣṇa (MBh).

गद्यमय (*gadyamaya*) M. "full of *gadya* or prose", Gaṇeśa (GS1). **गद्यमयी** (*gadyamayī*) F.

गन्धर्वी (*gandharvī*) F. "a celestial musician, a singer", Gāyatrī (GS4). **गन्धर्व** (*gandharva*) M.

गभीर (*gabhīra*) M. "deep, profound, grave", Viṣṇu (VS1). **गभीरा** (*gabhīrā*) F. Kumārī (KS4).

गम्भीरा (*gambhīrā*) F. "deep, endless", Lalitā (LS1). **गम्भीर** (*gambhīra*) M.

गरिष्ठ (*gariṣṭha*) M. "the greatest, the most venerable, the best *guru*", Gaṇeśa (GS1), Narasiṃha (NS). **गरिष्ठा** (*gariṣṭhā*) F. Durgā (DS3).

गरीयान् (*garīyān*) M. "greater, more honourable, more venerable", Gaṇeśa (GS1), Sūrya (SS1). **गरीयसी** (*garīyasī*) F. Gomātā (GS6).

गर्जित (*garjita*) M. "roaring, he who has roared", Narasiṃha

(NS). **गर्जिता** (*garjitā*) F.

गर्जिनी (*garjinī*) F. "she who roars, with a [loud] roar", a *śakti* (BrP). **गर्जी** (*garjī*) M.

गर्वनुद् (*garvanud*) MF. "remover of pride", Gaṇeśa (GS1).

गविष्ठ (*gaviṣṭha*) M. "situated among rays, the brightest", Sūrya (BhP). **गविष्ठा** (*gaviṣṭhā*) F.

गविष्ठिर (*gaviṣṭhira*) M. "firm in his speech", a *ṛṣi* (BrP). **गविष्ठिरा** (*gaviṣṭhirā*) F.

गविष्णु (*gaviṣṇu*) MF. "eager to go", one of the horses of the moon (BrP).

गवीशान (*gavīśāna*) M. "the ruler of *gos* (sense organs)", Gaṇeśa (GS1). **गवीशाना** (*gavīśānā*) F.

गवेशी (*gaveśī*) F. "the goddess of *gos* (cows, sense organs, and speech)", Rādhā (RS2). **गवेश** (*gaveśa*) M.

गह्वरी (*gahvarī*) F. "deep, impenetrable", Gāyatrī (GS4). **गह्वर** (*gahvara*) M.

गाधेय (*gādheya*) M. "the son of Gādhi", Viśvāmitra (MaP). **गाधेयी** (*gādheyī*) F. Satyavatī (MBh).

गान्धर्वी (*gāndharvī*) F. "a singer, daughter of *gandharvas*", daughter of Kaśyapa (BrP). **गान्धर्व** (*gāndharva*) M.

गायकेश (*gāyakeśa*) M. "lord of the singers", Gaṇeśa (GS1). **गायकेशी** (*gāyakeśī*) F.

गालव (*gālava*) M. "he who reaches (=knows) *gāla* (=*śāstra*)", a *ṛṣi* (BhP). **गालवा** (*gālavā*) F.

गिरिका (*girikā*) F. "she who calls to/from the mountain", a queen (MaP, VāP). **गिरिक** (*girika*) M. Śiva (ŚS4).

गिरित्र (*giritra*) M. "the protector of the mountains", Śiva (BhP). **गिरित्रा** (*giritrā*) F.

गीर्देव (*gīrdeva*) M. "the god of speech", Gaṇeśa (GS1). **गीर्देवी** (*gīrdevī*) F.

गीर्बाण (*gīrbāṇa*) M. "he whose arrow (=power) is his speech [alone]", a word for *devas* (AK). **गीर्बाणा** (*gīrbāṇā*) F.

गीर्वाणा (*gīrvāṇā*) F. "she who asks (=likes) speech", Annapūrṇā (AS). **गीर्वाण** (*gīrvāṇa*) M. a word for *devas* (AK).

गीष्पति (*gīṣpati*) M. "the lord of speech", Gaṇeśa (GS1).

गुडाकेश (*guḍākeśa*) M. "the master (=conqueror) of sleep and laziness", Arjuna (MBh). **गुडाकेशी** (*guḍākeśī*) F.

गुणाढ्या (*guṇāḍhyā*) F. "rich in virtues", Sītā (SS2). **गुणाढ्य** (*guṇāḍhya*) M.

गुणातीता (*guṇātītā*) F. "beyond the [three] *guṇas*", Gaṅgā (GS3). **गुणातीत** (*guṇātīta*) M.

गुण्या (*guṇyā*) F. "worthy of being described or praised", Gaṅgā (GS3). **गुण्य** (*guṇya*) M.

गुरुक्रम (*gurukrama*) M. "one with large steps or great acts", Gaṇeśa (GS1). **गुरुक्रमा** (*gurukramā*) F.

गुरुप्रीति (*gurupriti*) MF. "devoted to the guru", a *ṛṣi* (ViP).

गुरुवीत (*guruvīta*) M. "approved or liked by the guru", a *ṛṣi* (MaP). **गुरुवीता** (*guruvītā*) F.

गुर्वक्ष (*gurvakṣa*) M. "he whose eyes are on the guru (= he who waits upon the guru)", son of Bali (MaP). **गुर्वक्षी** (*gurvakṣī*) F.

गुर्वी (*gurvī*) F. "a female *guru*, venerable, mother", Gāyatrī (GS4), Gaṅgā (GS3). **गुरु** (*guru*) M.

गुहाम्बा (*guhāmbā*) F. "the mother of Guha (Kārttikeya)", Lalitā (LS1).

गुह्या (*guhyā*) F. "hidden or concealed [in the heart], mysterious, mystical", Gāyatrī (GS4). **गुह्य** (*guhya*) M. Viṣṇu (MBh).

गुह्येश (*guhyeśa*) M. "the lord who is concealed [in the heart]", Dattātreya (DS2). **गुह्येशी** (*guhyeśī*) F.

गृत्स (*gṛtsa*) M. "clever, judicious, wise, worthy of praise", Gaṇeśa (GS1), a *ṛṣi* (BrP). **गृत्सा** (*gṛtsā*) F.

गृत्समद (*gṛtsamada*) M. "he whose joy or pleasure is laudable", a *ṛṣi* (BhP). **गृत्समदा** (*gṛtsamadā*) F.

गृहेषु (*gṛheṣu*) MF. "seeking home", son of Sāvarṇi Manu (VāP).

गोखल (*gokhala*) M. "he who gathers *go* (Vedic speech)", disciple of Śākalya (BrP). **गोखला** (*gokhalā*) F.

गोचर (*gocara*) M. "to be perceived by the senses", Gaṇeśa (GS1). **गोचरा** (*gocarā*) F.

गोत्रकेतु (*gotraketu*) M. "the flag or banner of the *gotra*", Gaṇeśa (GS1).

गोत्रा (*gotrā*) F. "she who protects *go* (the cow or divine speech)", Gāyatrī (GS4), Yamunā (YS), Annapūrṇā (AS). **गोत्र** (*gotra*) M.

गोध्वज (*godhvaja*) M. "having a *go* (=bull) on his flag", Śiva (VāP).

गोपति (*gopati*) M. "lord of the cows and earth", Viṣṇu (VS1), Śiva (ŚS1).

गोपथ (*gopatha*) M. "he whose way has (=is full of) cows", Kṛṣṇa (KS2). **गोपथा** (*gopathā*) F.

गोपानन्द (*gopānanda*) M. "the delight of the *gopas* (cowherds)", Kṛṣṇa (RKS). **गोपानन्दा** (*gopānandā*) F.

गोपिनी (*gopinī*) F. "protectress, she who protects", Lakṣmī (LS2). **गोपी** (*gopī*) M.

गोपीश (*gopīśa*) M. "lord of the *gopīs* (cowherdesses)", Kṛṣṇa (BrP).

गोप्तव्या (*goptavyā*) F. "worth being preserved or guarded", Gāyatrī (GS4). **गोप्तव्य** (*goptavya*) M.

गोप्त्री (*goptrī*) F. "the protectress", Lalitā (LS1). **गोप्ता** (*goptā*) M.

गोभिल (*gobhila*) M. "he who divides *go* (the earth)", a *ṛṣi* (MaP).

गोमान् (*gomān*) M. "possessing *go* (cows, the earth, or rays)", Śiva (ŚS3). **गोमती** (*gomatī*) F.

गोहित (*gohita*) M. "beneficial for cows", Viṣṇu (VS1), Narasiṃha (NS). **गोहिता** (*gohitā*) F.

गौपायन (*gaupāyana*) M. "a descendant of Gopa", a *ṛṣi* (MaP). **गौपायनी** (*gaupāyanī*) F.

ग्रसिष्णु (*grasiṣṇu*) MF. "consuming [the world during *pralaya*]", Rāma (RS1), Hanumān (HS), Dattātreya (DS2).

ग्रहिल (*grahila*) M. "willing to accept", Kṛṣṇa (KS2). **ग्रहिला** (*grahilā*) F.

ग्रहेश (*graheśa*) M. "the lord of *grahas* or planets", Gaṇeśa (GS1). **ग्रहेशी** (*graheśī*) F.

ग्रहेषु (*graheṣu*) MF. "one whose arrows are seizing", son of Sāvarṇa Manu (BrP).

घर्मांशु (*gharmāṃśu*) M. "hot-rayed", Sūrya (SS1).

घस्मरा (*ghasmarā*) F. "she who devours or destroys [*pāpas*]", Gaṅgā (GS3). **घस्मर** (*ghasmara*) M.

घृताची (*ghṛtācī*) F. "reaching satisfaction with ghee", Gāyatrı (GS4), an Apsaras (MBh).

घृतायु (*ghṛtāyu*) MF. "desiring ghee [for oblations]", son of Purūravas (BrP).

घृतार्चिस् (*ghṛtārcis*) MF. "one whose effulgence [in this world] is ghee", Kṛshṇa/Vishṇu (MBh).

घृतेयु (*ghṛteyu*) MF. "desiring ghee [for oblations]", a king (VāP).

घोषा (*ghoṣā*) F. "possessing a proclamation [of praise] or sound", Gāyatrī (GS4), Gaṅgā (GS3). **घोष** (*ghoṣa*) M.

घोषिणी (*ghoṣiṇī*) F. "resonant, sonorous", Lakṣmī (LS2). **घोषी** (*ghoṣī*) M.

ङकार (*ṅakāra*) M. "causing (=bestowing) wishes", Gaṇeśa (GS2). **ङकारी** (*ṅakārī*) F. Kumārī (KS4).

चकिताक्ष (*cakitākṣa*) M. "with trembling (wavering) eyes", Kṛṣṇa (RKS). **चकिताक्षी** (*cakitākṣī*) F.

चक्रनाथा (*cakranāthā*) F. "goddess of the *cakra*", Lalitā (BrP). **चक्रनाथ** (*cakranātha*) M.

चक्रवर्तिनी (*cakravartinī*) F. "she whose nature is to reign all over the *cakra* (the earth)", Lalitā (BrP). **चक्रवर्ती** (*cakravartī*) M.

चक्रायुध (*cakrāyudha*) M. "he whose weapon is the *cakra*", Kṛṣṇa (MBh). **चक्रायुधा** (*cakrāyudhā*) F.

चक्रिका (*cakrikā*) F. "possessing the *cakra*", Lakṣmī (LS3). **चक्रिक** (*cakrika*) M.

चक्रिणी (*cakriṇī*) F. "possessing the *cakra*", Annapūrṇā (AS), Lalitā (BrP). **चक्री** (*cakrī*) M.

चक्रेश्वरी (*cakreśvarī*) F. "goddess of the *cakra*", Lalitā (BrP). **चक्रेश्वर** (*cakreśvara*) M. Śiva, whose beloved is Kumārī (KS4).

चक्षुष्मती (*cakṣuṣmatī*) F. "having praiseworthy (beautiful) eyes", Lakṣmī (LS3). **चक्षुष्मान्** (*cakṣuṣmān*) M.

चक्षुष्य (*cakṣuṣya*) M. "pleasing for the eyes, beautiful/ handsome", Śiva (ŚS3). **चक्षुष्या** (*cakṣuṣyā*) F.

चन्दिला (*candilā*) F. "possessing the moon", Gāyatrī (GS4). **चन्दिल** (*candila*) M.

चन्द्रकेतु (*candraketu*) MF. "having the [sign of] the moon on his flag", son of Lakṣmaṇa (BrP).

चन्द्रभ (*candrabha*) M. "having the splendour or beauty of the moon", a warrior of Skanda (MBh). **चन्द्रभा** (*candrabhā*) F. a river (MaP).

चन्द्राभा (*candrābhā*) F. "having the splendour or beauty of the moon", Lakṣmī (LS2). **चन्द्राभ** (*candrābha*) M.

चरन्त (*caranta*) M. "he who moves [swiftly]", son of Ārṣṭiṣeṇa (VāP). **चरन्ती** (*carantī*) F.

चरिष्णु (*cariṣṇu*) MF. "one who moves (=makes efforts) [constantly]", son of Sāvarṇi Manu (MaP, VāP).

चर्चिका (*carcikā*) F. "she who anoints, she who repeats [a mantra]", Sītā (SS2), Caṇḍikā or Durgā (TK). **चर्चक** (*carcaka*) M.

चर्चिता (*carcitā*) F. "anointed, perfumed, sought, desired", Gāyatrī (GS4). **चर्चित** (*carcita*) M.

चाक्षुष (*cākṣuṣa*) M. "depending on the eye (=vision or

knowledge)", the sixth Manu (BhP). **चाक्षुषी** (*cākṣuṣī*) F.

चातका (*cātakā*) F. "she who asks for [*bhakti* from her devotees]", Gāyatrī (GS4). **चातक** (*cātaka*) M.

चापिनी (*cāpinī*) F. "bearing a bow", Annapūrṇā (AS), Bhavānī (BS). **चापी** (*cāpī*) M.

चारुक (*cāruka*) M. "sounding well, having a good voice or speech", a Yādava prince (ViP). **चारुका** (*cārukā*) F.

चारुकेशी (*cārukeśī*) F. "having beautiful hair", an Apsaras (MaP). **चारुकेश** (*cārukeśa*) M.

चारुदेष्ण (*cārudeṣṇa*) M. "he whose gifts are pleasing or good", son of Kṛṣṇa (MBh, BhP). **चारुदेष्णा** (*cārudeṣṇā*) F.

चारुविद्य (*cāruvidya*) M. "he whose learning is delightful", son of Kṛṣṇa (BrP). **चारुविद्या** (*cāruvidyā*) F.

चार्वङ्गी (*cārvaṅgī*) F. "with beautiful limbs or body", Gaṅgā (GS3). **चार्वङ्ग** (*cārvaṅga*) M.

चिकित्वान् (*cikitvān*) M. "learned, wise, knowledgeable", a *deva* in Svārociṣa *manvantara* (BrP). **चिकित्वती** (*cikitvatī*) F.

चित्रकेतु (*citraketu*) MF. "having a bright banner or flag", son of Garuḍa (MBh), son of Kṛṣṇa (BhP).

चित्रवती (*citravatī*) F. "wonderful, astonishing", a princess (BrP). **चित्रवान्** (*citravān*) M.

चित्रिणी (*citriṇī*) F. "wonderful, variegated", Bhavānī (BS). **चित्री** (*citrī*) M.

चिद्रूप (*cidrūpa*) M. "kind-hearted, wise, intelligent, conscious", Rāma (RS1), Narasiṃha (NS). **चिद्रूपा** (*cidrūpā*) F.

चिन्मात्र (*cinmātra*) M. "consisting of consciousness alone", Dattātreya (DS2). **चिन्मात्रा** (*cinmātrā*) F.

चेकितान (*cekitāna*) M. "sentient, wise, knowing", Śiva (ŚS1). **चेकिताना** (*cekitānā*) F. Sītā (SS2).

च्यवन (*cyavana*) M. "flowing [with compassion]", Hanumān (HS). **च्यवनी** (*cyavanī*) F.

छत्रिका (*chatrikā*) F. "she who covers (=protects)", a *śakti* (BrP). **छत्रक** (*chatraka*) M.

छत्रेशी (*chatreśī*) F. "the goddess of parasols", similar to name *chatreśvarī* of Gāyatrī (GS4). **छत्रेश** (*chatreśa*) M.

छन्दोमय (*chandomaya*) M. "consisting of Vedas", Kṛṣṇa (KS1). **छन्दोमयी** (*chandomayī*) F.

छान्दसी (*chāndasī*) F. "related to the Vedas", Lakṣmī (LS2). **छान्दस** (*chāndasa*) M.

जगती (*jagatī*) F. "she who moves [everywhere]", Gāyatrī (GS4). **जगन्** (*jagan*) M.

जगदन्त (*jagadanta*) M. "he who ends he world", Hanumān (HS). **जगदन्ता** (*jagadantā*) F.

जगद्धर (*jagaddhara*) M. "bearing or supporting the world", Viṣṇu (VS1, VS2). **जगद्धरा** (*jagaddharā*) F.

जगद्वसु (*jagadvasu*) M. "wealth of the worlds", Kṛṣṇa (KS2).

जगन्मयी (*jaganmayī*) F. "containing the whole world or universe", Gāyatrī (GS4). **जगन्मय** (*jaganmaya*) M. Kṛṣṇa (KS1), Gaṇeśa (GS2).

जनित्री (*janitrī*) F. "she who gives birth, the mother", Gāyatrī (GS4). **जनिता** (*janitā*) M.

जन्मदा (*janmadā*) F. "she who gives birth", Annapūrṇā (AS). **जन्मद** (*janmada*) M.

जपित (*japita*) M. "he who (=whose name) is repeated or chanted", Narasiṃha (NS). **जपिता** (*japitā*) F.

जप्य (*japya*) M. "he who (=whose name) is worth repeating or chanting", Narasiṃha (NS), Gaṇeśa (GS2). **जप्या** (*japyā*) F. Gaṅgā (GS3).

जयत्सेन (*jayatsena*) M. "with a victorious army", a king (MBh). **जयत्सेना** (*jayatsenā*) F.

जयदा (*jayadā*) F. "bestower of victory", Annapūrṇā (AS), Sītā (SS2), Bhavānī (BS). **जयद** (*jayada*) M. a king (VāP).

जयसेन (*jayasena*) M. "he whose army exists for victory [alone]", a king (BhP). **जयसेना** (*jayasenā*) F.

जयस्था (*jayasthā*) F. "situated in [every] victory", Annapūrṇā (AS). **जयस्थ** (*jayastha*) M.

जयित्री (*jayitrī*) F. "victorious, she who wins", Kumārī (KS4). **जयिता** (*jayitā*) M.

जलशायी (*jalaśāyī*) M. "he who sleeps in the waters", Viṣṇu

(MaP). **जलशायिनी** (*jalaśāyinī*) F.

जलस्था (*jalasthā*) F. "situated in (=pervading) water", Bhavānī (BS). **जलस्थ** (*jalastha*) M.

जलेयु (*jaleyu*) MF. "wishing for water (=a place near a river)", a king (BhP).

जविष्ठ (*javiṣṭha*) M. "the quickest, faster than all", a *deva* (BrP). **जविष्ठा** (*javiṣṭhā*) F.

जागरिणी (*jāgariṇī*) F. "awake (=enlightened)", Lalitā (LS1). **जागरी** (*jāgarī*) M.

जिगीषु (*jigīṣu*) MF. "desirous of victory, striving to excel", a *deva* (BrP).

जितमन्यु (*jitamanyu*) MF. "one who has conquered anger", Viṣṇu (VS1).

जितव्रत (*jitavrata*) M. "he who has conquered (=fulfilled) his vows", a king (MBh). **जितव्रता** (*jitavratā*) F.

जितामित्र (*jitāmitra*) M. "conqueror of enemies", Viṣṇu (VS1), Rāma (RS1), Hanumān (HS). **जितामित्रा** (*jitāmitrā*) F. Sarasvatī (SS3).

जितारि (*jitāri*) MF. "conqueror of enemies", Rāma (RS1), Narasiṃha (NS).

जित्वरी (*jitvarī*) F. "victorious, triumphant", Sītā (SS2). **जित्वर** (*jitvara*) M.

जीविनी (*jīvinī*) F. "alive, thriving", a *śakti* (BrP). **जीवी** (*jīvī*) M.

जेत्री (*jetrī*) F. "winning, victorious", Gāyatrī (GS4). **जेता** (*jetā*) M. one of the *amitābhas* (BrP).

जैगीषव्य (*jaigīṣavya*) M. "descendant of Jigīṣu", a *ṛṣi* (MBh, BhP). **जैगीषव्यायणी** (*jaigīṣavyāyaṇī*) F.

जैत्री (*jaitrī*) F. "victorious, triumphant, superior", Annapūrṇā (AS), Sītā (SS2). **जैत्र** (*jaitra*) M. servant of Kṛṣṇa (BhP).

ज्या (*jyā*) F. "the earth, a mother", Gaṅgā (GS3).

ज्यायान् (*jyāyān*) M. "elder, senior, superior, more praiseworthy", Sūrya (SS1). **ज्यायसी** (*jyāyasī*) F.

ज्येष्ठराज (*jyeṣṭharāja*) M. "he who shines (=stands out) among the most praiseworthy", Brahmaṇaspati (ṚVŚ, KYT), Gaṇeśa (GS5).

ज्येष्ठा (*jyeṣṭhā*) F. "eldest, best, most excellent or praiseworthy", Gaṅgā (GS3), Lakṣmī (LS2). **ज्येष्ठ** (*jyeṣṭha*) M.

ज्योतिष्मती (*jyotiṣmatī*) F. "bright, shining, resplendent", Lakṣmī (LS2). **ज्योतिष्मान्** (*jyotiṣmān*) M.

ज्योत्स्नी (*jyotsnī*) F. "a night with moonlight, possessing moonlight", a *śakti* (BrP).

ज्वलन्ती (*jvalantī*) F. "burning, blazing (=shining or brilliant)", Lakṣmī (LS3). **ज्वलन्** (*jvalan*) M.

ज्वालिनी (*jvālinī*) F. "flaming, dazzling", Lakṣmī (LS2). **ज्वाली** (*jvālī*) M.

झङ्करी (*jhaṅkarī*) F. "she who makes the *jhaṅ* (jingling or clanking sound), a dancer", Kumārī (KS4). **झङ्कर** (*jhaṅkara*) M.

झर्झरी (*jharjharī*) M. "having (=playing) the drum", Śiva (ŚS4). **झर्झरिणी** (*jharjhariṇī*) F.

झषाक्षी (*jhaṣākṣī*) F. "fish-eyed, she whose eyes are [beautiful] like those of a fish", Mīnākṣī Devī. **झषाक्ष** (*jhaṣākṣa*) M.

ञभुजा (*ñabhujā*) F. "holding the parrot in one arm (hand)", Gāyatrī (GS4).

ञरूपा (*ñarūpā*) F. "having the form of bulls and oxen", Gāyatrī (GS4). **ञरूप** (*ñarūpa*) M.

टङ्कहस्ता (*ṭaṅkahastā*) F. "with a sword in her hand", a *śakti* (BrP). **टङ्कहस्त** (*ṭaṅkahasta*) M.

टङ्कारिणी (*ṭaṅkāriṇī*) F. "surprising, wonderful", a *śakti* (BrP). **टङ्कारी** (*ṭaṅkārī*) M.

डामरेश (*ḍāmareśa*) M. "lord of the *Ḍāmara-Tantra*", Mṛtyuñjaya (MS1). **डामरेशी** (*ḍāmareśī*) F.

ढुण्ढि (*ḍhuṇḍhi*) M. "he who finds [everything]", Gaṇeśa (ŚK, VK1).

तटस्था (*taṭasthā*) F. "indifferent [to *dvandvas* like pleasure and pain]", Yamunā (YS). **तटस्थ** (*taṭastha*) M.

तनित (*tanita*) M. "made to spread or pervade", Sūrya (SS1). **तनिता** (*tanitā*) F.

तनीयसी (*tanīyasī*) F. "more slender, very thin or light", Lalitā

(LS1). **तनीयान्** (*tanīyān*) M.

तनुत्र (*tanutra*) M. "he who protects the body [of a devotee]", Narasiṃha (NS). **तनुत्रा** (*tanutrā*) F.

तन्त्रिणी (*tantriṇī*) F. "knowing Tantra, a female musician", Annapūrṇā (AS). **तन्त्री** (*tantrī*) M.

तपस्विनी (*tapasvinī*) F. "austere, devout, practising askesis", Sītā (SS2), Bhavānī (BS). **तपस्वी** (*tapasvī*) M.

तपस्वीश (*tapasvīśa*) M. "the lord of ascetics", Rāma (RS1). **तपस्वीशी** (*tapasvīśī*) F.

तपोत्सुक (*tapotsuka*) M. "eager for *tapas* (austerities or askesis)", a *brāhmaṇa* (MaP). **तपोत्सुका** (*tapotsukā*) F.

तपोद्युति (*tapodyuti*) MF. "one whose brilliance comes from *tapas*", son of Tāmasa Manu (MaP).

तपोधन (*tapodhana*) M. "rich in *tapas*", a *ṛṣi* (BrP). **तपोधना** (*tapodhanā*) F.

तपोनुदा (*taponudā*) F. "she who expels pain or suffering", Lakṣmī (LS2). **तपोनुद** (*taponuda*) M.

तपोमय (*tapomaya*) M. "consisting of (=practising) *tapas* (askesis)", Śiva (ŚS1). **तपोमयी** (*tapomayī*) F. Gaṅgā (GS3).

तपोवास (*tapovāsa*) M. "the abode of heat, light, or asceticism", Rāma (RS1). **तपोवासा** (*tapovāsā*) F.

तमोहर (*tamohara*) M. "the remover of [spiritual] darkness", Śiva (ŚS3). **तमोहरा** (*tamoharā*) F.

तरक्ष (*tarakṣa*) M. "he who destroys the path or movement [of the *asuras*]", Narasiṃha (NS).

तरण्य (*taraṇya*) M. "he who moves quickly", a *gandharva* (VāP). **तरण्या** (*taraṇyā*) F.

तरस्वी (*tarasvī*) M. "having speed or strength, swift, powerful", Narasiṃha (NS). **तरस्विनी** (*tarasvinī*) F.

तर्पणी (*tarpaṇī*) F. "the means of satisfaction or *tarpaṇa*", Gaṅgā (GS3). **तर्पण** (*tarpaṇa*) M.

तापनीय (*tāpanīya*) M. "golden, worthy of being heated (=tested, like gold is)", disciple of Yājñavalkya (BrP). **तापनीया** (*tāpanīyā*) F.

तार्किकी (*tārkikī*) F. "philosopher, logician", Annapūrṇā (AS). **तार्किक** (*tārkika*) M.

तार्क्ष्य (*tārkṣya*) M. "son of Tārkṣa (=Kaśyapa)", Garuḍa (MBh). **तार्क्षी** (*tārkṣī*) F.

तिग्मांशु (*tigmāṃśu*) M. "hot-rayed", Sūrya (SS1).

तितिक्षा (*titikṣā*) F. "patient, forbearing, enduring", Yamunā (YS). **तितिक्ष** (*titikṣa*) M.

तितिक्षु (*titikṣu*) MF. "patient, forbearing, enduring", a king (BhP).

तीव्र (*tīvra*) M. "intense, hot, endless", Sūrya (SS1). **तीव्रा** (*tīvrā*) F. a *śakti* (BrP), Durgā (DS3), Gāyatrī (GS4).

तुक्षय (*tukṣaya*) M. "he who is the end of *tus* (=expressions of doubt)", a *ṛṣi* (BrP). **तुक्षया** (*tukṣayā*) F.

तुर्या (*turyā*) F. "the fourth [state of consciousness], superior power", Lalitā (LS1), Gaṅgā (GS3). **तुर्य** (*turya*) M.

तुर्वसु (*turvasu*) MF. "one whose wealth is speed, quick", son of Yayāti (BhP).

तुलजा (*tulajā*) F. "born under *tulā* (Libra)", Annapūrṇā (AS). **तुलज** (*tulaja*) M.

तुल्यार्चि (*tulyārci*) MF. "one whose brilliance is comparable [to that of gods]", a king (VāP).

तुष्टिदा (*tuṣṭidā*) F. "she who gives satisfaction or pleasure", Gaṅgā (GS3), Bhavānī (BS). **तुष्टिद** (*tuṣṭida*) M.

तुष्टिमान् (*tuṣṭimān*) M. "satisfied", son of Ugrasena (BhP). **तुष्टिमती** (*tuṣṭimatī*) F.

तेजस्कर (*tejaskara*) M. "the cause of valour, giving valour", Śiva (ŚS3). **तेजस्करी** (*tejaskarī*) F. Sarasvatī (SS3).

तेजिष्ठ (*tejiṣṭha*) M. "most brilliant or powerful", Dattātreya (DS2). **तेजिष्ठा** (*tejiṣṭhā*) F.

तेजोधर (*tejodhara*) M. "bearing *tejas* (brilliance)", Rāma (RS1). **तेजोधरा** (*tejodharā*) F.

तेजोमय (*tejomaya*) M. "made of light or power, very brilliant or powerful", Śiva (ŚS3). **तेजोमयी** (*tejomayī*) F.

तेजोरश्मि (*tejoraśmi*) MF. "one whose rays/brilliance are/is like that of *tejas* (Sūrya)", a *deva* (BrP).

तेजोरूप (*tejorūpa*) M. "having the form of light", Kṛṣṇa (KS1). **तेजोरूपा** (*tejorūpā*) F.

तेजोवती (*tejovatī*) F. "possessing splendour or brilliance", Lalitā (LS1). **तेजोवान्** (*tejovān*) M.

तैजस (*taijasa*) M. "bright, passionate, powerful", a king (VāP). **तैजसी** (*taijasī*) F.

तोयेशी (*toyeśī*) F. "the goddess of water", Gaṅgā (GS3). **तोयेश** (*toyeśa*) M.

तोषिणी (*toṣiṇī*) F. "gladdening, satisfying, pleasing", Lakṣmī (LS2). **तोषी** (*toṣī*) M.

त्रयी (*trayī*) F. "[being or pervading] the three Vedas", Annapūrṇā (AS).

त्रयीमय (*trayīmaya*) M. "consisting of (or being) the three Vedas", Viṣṇu (VS2). **त्रयीमयी** (*trayīmayī*) F.

त्रासन (*trāsana*) M. "frightening, terrifying", Śiva (ŚS1). **त्रासनी** (*trāsanī*) F.

त्रिकर (*trikara*) M. "the cause of the three (three *guṇas—sattva*, *rajas*, and *tamas*)", Gaṇeśa (GS2). **त्रिकरी** (*trikarī*) F.

त्रिचक्ष (*tricakṣa*) M. "seeing the three [times—past, present, and future]", a king (VāP). **त्रिचक्षा** (*tricakṣā*) F.

त्रितत्त्वा (*tritattvā*) F. "having three entities (*sattva*, *rajas*, and *tamas*)", Sītā (SS2). **त्रितत्त्व** (*tritattva*) M.

त्रिदशा (*tridaśā*) F. "always in the third state (youth)",

Annapūrṇā (AS). **त्रिदश** (*tridaśa*) M.

त्रिदशेश (*tridaśeśa*) M. "the lord of the *tridaśa* (gods)", Kṛṣṇa (MBh). **त्रिदशेशी** (*tridaśeśī*) F.

त्रिदिवा (*tridivā*) F. "possessing *svarga*", Annapūrṇā (AS). **त्रिदिव** (*tridiva*) M.

त्रिधन्वा (*tridhanvā*) MF. "having three bows", a king (VāP).

त्रिधा (*tridhā*) F. "threefold, having three aspects or forms (*kṣara, akṣara,* and *puruṣottama*)", Durgā (DS3), Lakṣmī (LS2), Yamunā (YS).

त्रिधातु (*tridhātu*) M. "nourishing the three *dhātus* (*vāta, pitta,* and *kapha*), having three components (the three sounds of OM—*a, u,* and *m*)", Kṛṣṇa (MBh), Gaṇeśa (TK).

त्रिधामा (*tridhāmā*) MF. "possessing three abodes (the three sounds of OM—*a, u,* and *m*)", Viṣṇu (VS2), Śiva (ŚS3). **त्रिधाम्नी** (*tridhāmnī*) F. Annapūrṇā (AS).

त्रिपदा (*tripadā*) F. "having three [prosodic] feet, the *gāyatrī* metre", Gāyatrī (GS4). **त्रिपात्** (*tripāt*) M.

त्रिपदी (*tripadī*) F. "with movement across three [realms] (*svarga*, earth, and *pātāla*)", Gaṅgā (GS3).

त्रिभानु (*tribhānu*) MF. "one whose brilliance is [spread] in the three [*lokas*]", a king (BhP).

त्रियुग (*triyuga*) M. "pervading or appearing in the three *yugas* (*Satya, Tretā,* and *Dvāpara*)", Śiva (ŚS1), Kṛṣṇa (MBh). **त्रियुगा**

(*triyugā*) F.

त्रियुता (*triyutā*) F. "endowed with three [sounds of OM]", Gāyatrī (GS4). **त्रियुत** (*triyuta*) M.

त्रिलक्ष्या (*trilakṣyā*) F. "seen (=present) in three [times], worthy of being seen (=known) in three ([realms]—*svarga*, earth, and *pātāla*)", Gaṅgā (GS3). **त्रिलक्ष्य** (*trilakṣya*) M.

त्रिविद्य (*trividya*) M. "he whose *vidyā* (learning or nature) is threefold", Śiva (ŚS3). **त्रिविद्या** (*trividyā*) F.

त्रिविधा (*trividhā*) F. "of three kinds", Gāyatrī (GS4), Lakṣmī (LS2), Annapūrṇā (AS). **त्रिविध** (*trividha*) M.

त्रिशक्ति (*triśakti*) MF. "having three powers (powers of creation, protection, and destruction), [the source of] the power of the three (Brahmā, Viṣṇu, and Śiva)", Bhavānī (BS).

त्रिशिख (*triśikha*) M. "having three tufts or flames", Indra of the fourth *manvantara* (BhP). **त्रिशिखा** (*triśikhā*) F. Lakṣmī (LS3).

त्रिशुक्ल (*triśukla*) M. "with three pure entities (body, mind, and speech)", Śiva (ŚS1). **त्रिशुक्ला** (*triśuklā*) F.

त्रिसन्ध्या (*trisandhyā*) F. "having the form of the three *sandhyās*", Gāyatrī (GS4), Bhavānī (BS), Sītā (SS2). **त्रिसन्ध्य** (*trisandhya*) M.

त्रिस्था (*tristhā*) F. "present in three [times—past, present, and future], present in three [worlds]", Annapūrṇā (AS), Lalitā (LS1). **त्रिस्थ** (*tristha*) M.

त्रैपुर (*traipura*) M. "ruler of three cities", *avatāra* of Viṣṇu (MaP). **त्रैपुरी** (*traipurī*) F.

त्रैविद्या (*traividyā*) F. "well-versed in three Vedas", Annapūrṇā (AS). **त्रैविद्य** (*traividya*) M.

त्र्यक्ष (*tryakṣa*) M. "having three eyes (*akṣis*), he whose sense organs (*akṣas*) are [active] in three [times or realms]", Śiva (ŚS1). **त्र्यक्षा** (*tryakṣā*) F. "she whose sense organs are [active] in three [times or realms]", Annapūrṇā (AS).

त्र्यक्षर (*tryakṣara*) M. "imperishable in three [times—past, present, and future], having three syllables (*a*, *u*, and *m* of OM)", Śiva (LiP), Sūrya (SS1). **त्र्यक्षरी** (*tryakṣarī*) F. "the collection of three *bījākṣaras* [of *vāk*, *kāma*, and *śakti*]", Lalitā (LS1).

त्र्यम्बका (*tryambakā*) F. "having three eyes (the sun, the moon, and fire), mother of three (Brahmā, Viṣṇu, and Rudra)", Lalitā (LS1). **त्र्यम्बक** (*tryambaka*) M. Śiva (ŚS4).

त्विषि (*tviṣi*) F. "[possessing] beauty or lustre", mother of Budha (BrP).

त्विषिमान् (*tviṣimān*) M. "possessing beauty, lustre, or rays of light", son of Dharma (VāP). **त्विषिमती** (*tviṣimatī*) F.

थात्कारी (*thātkārī*) F. "she who makes the *thāt* sound [to protect from fear]", Gāyatrī (GS4). **थात्कार** (*thātkāra*) M.

थारवा (*thāravā*) F. "she whose sound (=voice or speech) protects from fear", Gāyatrī (GS4). **थारव** (*thārava*) M.

दक्षजा (*dakṣajā*) F. "the daughter of Dakṣa", Durgā (DS3).

दक्षसू (*dakṣasū*) F. "the daughter of Dakṣa", Durgā (DS1).

दक्षेज्या (*dakṣejyā*) F. "worthy of being worshipped by Dakṣa", Durgā (DS1). **दक्षेज्य** (*dakṣejya*) M.

दयात्मिका (*dayātmikā*) F. "she whose nature is compassion, compassion itself", Durgā (DS1). **दयात्मक** (*dayātmaka*) M.

दयार्द्रा (*dayārdrā*) F. "moist with compassion, compassionate", Durgā (DS1). **दयार्द्र** (*dayārdra*) M.

दरघ्नी (*daraghnī*) F. "the slayer of fear", Durgā (DS1). **दरघ्न** (*daraghna*) M.

दात्री (*dātrī*) F. "giver, bestower", Durgā (DS1), Gaṅgā (GS3). **दाता** (*dātā*) M.

दान्त (*dānta*) M. "self-controlled, liberal", Rāma (RS1), Kṛṣṇa (KS1). **दान्ता** (*dāntā*) F.

दायिनी (*dāyinī*) F. "giving, bestowing, munificent", Lakṣmī (LS2). **दायी** (*dāyī*) M.

दाशार्ह (*dāśārha*) M. "worthy of donations (=offerings)", Viṣṇu (VS1), Kṛṣṇa (MBh). **दाशार्हा** (*dāśārhā*) F.

दाहिका (*dāhikā*) F. "burning [impurities]", Durgā (DS1). **दाहक** (*dāhaka*) M.

दिक्पति (*dikpati*) M. "lord of the directions", a *deva* (BrP, VāP).

दिगन्तरा (*digantarā*) F. "[possessing or pervading] the space of

[all] directions", Durgā (DS1). **दिगन्तर** (*digantara*) M.

दिवञ्जय (*divañjaya*) M. "the conqueror of *svarga*", a king (BrP, VāP). **दिवञ्जया** (*divañjayā*) F.

दिवस्पति (*divaspati*) M. "lord of the sky or *svarga*", Indra (AK), Sūrya (SS1), Rāma (RS1), Kṛṣṇa (KS2).

दिवाक (*divāka*) M. "he who speaks during the day", a king (BhP). **दिवाका** (*divākā*) F.

दिविरथ (*diviratha*) M. "he whose chariot goes till the sky or *svarga*", a king (BhP). **दिविरथा** (*divirathā*) F.

दिविषदा (*diviṣadā*) F. "dwelling in the sky or *svarga*", Gāyatrī (GS4). **दिविषद्** (*diviṣad*) M.

दिविस्पृक् (*divispṛk*) MF. "touching the sky or *svarga*", Viṣṇu (VS1).

दिव्यमान (*divyamāna*) M. "he whose measure (=extent of greatness) is divine", a *deva* (BrP). **दिव्यमाना** (*divyamānā*) F.

दीप्तकेतु (*dīptaketu*) MF. "having a brilliant flag or banner", son of the ninth Manu Dakṣa Sāvarṇi (BhP).

दीप्तास्या (*dīptāsyā*) F. "she whose face is beaming or radiant", Durgā (DS3). **दीप्तास्य** (*dīptāsya*) M.

दीप्तिकेतु (*dīptiketu*) MF. "one whose banner is light (radiance) itself", son of Sāvarṇa Manu (BrP).

दीर्घाङ्गी (*dīrghāṅgī*) F. "long-limbed", Durgā (DS1). **दीर्घाङ्ग** (*dīrghāṅga*) M.

दुरत्यया (*duratyayā*) F. "difficult to cross over or overcome", Sītā (SS2). **दुरत्यय** (*duratyaya*) M.

दुरासदा (*durāsadā*) F. "difficult to attain or reach", Durgā (DS1), Gaṅgā (GS3), Annapūrṇā (AS). **दुरासद** (*durāsada*) M. Rāma (RS1), Kṛṣṇa (KS1).

दुर्गमा (*durgamā*) F. "difficult to reach or understand", Durgā (DS1), Gaṅgā (GS3), Lalitā (LS1), Bhavānī (BS). **दुर्गम** (*durgama*) M. Viṣṇu (VS1), Śiva (ŚS3).

दुर्जया (*durjayā*) F. "difficult to conquer, invincible", Durgā (DS1), Lakṣmī (LS2). **दुर्जय** (*durjaya*) M. Viṣṇu (VS1), Śiva (ŚS3).

दुर्दम (*durdama*) M. "difficult to be tame or subdue", son of Vasudeva (BrP). **दुर्दमा** (*durdamā*) F.

दुर्ध्येया (*durdhyeyā*) F. "[present in] the interior of directions or space", Durgā (DS1). **दुर्ध्येय** (*durdhyeya*) M.

दुर्वारा (*durvārā*) F. "difficult to stop or restrain", Sītā (SS2). **दुर्वार** (*durvāra*) M.

दृग्रूपा (*dṛgrūpā*) F. "having the form of vision, vision itself", Durgā (DS1). **दृग्रूप** (*dṛgrūpa*) M.

देवज (*devaja*) M. "born from a *deva,* divine", a king (BhP). **देवजा** (*devajā*) F.

देवद्युम्न (*devadyumna*) M. "having the *dyumna* (splendour, glory, lustre, power, opulence, or inspiration) of gods", a king (BhP). **देवद्युम्ना** (*devadyumnā*) F.

देवमित्र (*devamitra*) M. "friend of the gods", disciple of Maṇḍūkeya (BhP). **देवमित्रा** (*devamitrā*) F.

देवयु (*devayu*) MF. "one who reaches/understands/knows the gods, virtuous", used for *camasa* (ṚVŚ).

देवरात (*devarāta*) M. "protected by the gods", *ṛṣi* Śunaḥśepha (BhP). **देवराता** (*devarātā*) F.

देवरीति (*devarīti*) MF. "having the ways and manner of the gods", Gāyatrī (GS4).

देवश्रवस् (*devaśravas*) MF. "one whose fame is like that of the gods", a king (BhP).

देवहूति (*devahūti*) F. "she who is enlightened by *deva* (=Kapila)", mother of Kapila (BhP).

देवहोत्र (*devahotra*) M. "he who has offerings for *devas*", father of Yogeśvara incarnation (BhP). **देवहोत्रा** (*devahotrā*) F.

देवातिथि (*devātithi*) MF. "guest of the gods", a king (BhP).

देवेज्या (*devejyā*) F. "worthy of being worshipped by the gods", Durgā (DS1). **देवेज्य** (*devejya*) M.

द्युक्ष (*dyukṣa*) M. "he who resides in *svarga*, he who resides or moves with light or brilliance", used for Varuṇa, Aryamā, Indra, Agni, and Soma (ṚVŚ). **द्युक्षा** (*dyukṣā*) F.

द्युतय (*dyutaya*) M. "shining, brilliant", a *deva* (BrP). **द्युतया** (*dyutayā*) F.

द्युतिकर (*dyutikara*) M. "the cause of brilliance, shining, brilliant", Śiva (ŚS3). **द्युतिकरी** (*dyutikarī*) F.

द्युतिमान् (*dyutimān*) M. "resplendent, radiant, brilliant", Sūrya (SS1), Rāma (RS1). **द्युतिमती** (*dyutimatī*) F.

द्युनदी (*dyunadī*) F. "the river of *svarga*", Gaṅgā (GS3).

द्युमणि (*dyumaṇi*) MF. "the jewel of the sky (Sūrya)", Śiva (ŚS3).

द्युमत्सेन (*dyumatsena*) M. "he whose army is strong", a king (BhP). **द्युमत्सेना** (*dyumatsenā*) F.

द्युमान् (*dyumān*) M. "bright, brilliant, strong", son of Vasiṣṭha (BhP). **द्युमती** (*dyumatī*) F.

द्युवीर (*dyuvīra*) M. "brave in the sky, a sky warrior". **द्युवीरा** (*dyuvīrā*) F.

द्योत (*dyota*) M. "he who shines", Sūrya (SS1). **द्योता** (*dyotā*) F.

द्योतन (*dyotana*) M. "bright, shining, resplendent", Sūrya (SS1). **द्योतना** (*dyotanā*) F.

द्राघीयसी (*drāghīyasī*) F. "longer, higher, very long or high", Gaṅgā (GS3). **द्राघीयान्** (*drāghīyān*) M.

द्राविणी (*drāviṇī*) F. "flowing, melting, moving", Gaṅgā (GS3). **द्रावी** (*drāvī*) M.

द्रुति (*druti*) F. "quick (or quickness), speedy (or speediness)", a queen (BhP).

द्वारेशी (*dvāreśī*) F. "the goddess of the door (=gate) [to *mokṣa*]", Durgā (DS3). **द्वारेश** (*dvāreśa*) M.

द्वैमातुर (*dvaimātura*) M. "having two mothers (a natural mother and a step/foster-mother)", Gaṇeśa (GS2). **द्वैमातुरी** (*dvaimāturī*) F.

धनदा (*dhanadā*) F. "bestower of wealth, she who grants prosperity", Gāyatrī (GS4), Lakṣmī (LS2), Gaṅgā (GS3). **धनद** (*dhanada*) M.

धनायु (*dhanāyu*) MF. "seeking riches", son of Purūravas (MaP).

धनुर्वेद (*dhanurveda*) M. "knower of the art of archery (or war)", Viṣṇu (VS1), Śiva (ŚS3), Rāma (RS1), Gaṇeśa (GS2). **धनुर्वेदा** (*dhanurvedā*) F.

धराधीश (*dharādhīśa*) M. "the supreme lord of the earth", Rāma (RS1). **धराधीशी** (*dharādhīśī*) F.

धर्मग (*dharmaga*) M. "he who follows (=knows) *dharma*", Dattātreya (DS2). **धर्मगा** (*dharmagā*) F.

धर्मदा (*dharmadā*) F. "she who bestows [the knowledge of] *dharma*", Bhavānī (BS). **धर्मद** (*dharmada*) M.

धर्मिष्ठ (*dharmiṣṭha*) M. "supremely virtuous, best among those who have *dharma*", Gaṇeśa (GS2). **धर्मिष्ठा** (*dharmiṣṭhā*) F.

धर्मेयु (*dharmeyu*) MF. "desirous of *dharma*", a king (BhP).

धर्मेशी (*dharmeśī*) F. "the goddess of *dharma*", Gaṅgā (GS3). **धर्मेश** (*dharmeśa*) M.

धर्मेषु (*dharmeṣu*) MF. "one whose arrows (weapon) are (is) *dharma*", a king (ViP).

धात्रीश (*dhātrīśa*) M. "the lord of Brahmā (*dhātṛ*) or the earth (*dhātrī*)", Śiva (ŚS3). **धात्रीशी** (*dhātrīśī*) F.

धावनी (*dhāvanī*) F. "she who cleanses or purifies", Gaṅgā (GS3). **धावन** (*dhāvana*) M.

धियान्त (*dhiyānta*) M. "he who binds [his opponents] using his intellect", a king (VāP). **धियान्ता** (*dhiyāntā*) F.

धिष्णु (*dhiṣṇu*) MF. "sounding [well]", son of Aṅgiras (VāP).

धीमान् (*dhīmān*) M. "intelligent, wise, possessing intellect", Viṣṇu (VS2). **धीमती** (*dhīmatī*) F. Pārvatī (PS), Sītā (SS2), Durgā (DS4).

धुरन्धर (*dhurandhara*) M. "bearing a burden", Narasiṃha (NS). **धुरन्धरा** (*dhurandharā*) F. Lakṣmī (LS2), Sītā (SS2).

धुर्य (*dhurya*) M. "able to bear a burden, chief, foremost", Viṣṇu (VS1), Rāma (RS1). **धुर्या** (*dhuryā*) F. Gaṅgā (GS3).

धृतेयु (*dhṛteyu*) MF. "desiring resolve or steadiness", a king (ViP).

धौम्य (*dhaumya*) M. "a descendant of Dhūma", *purohita* of Pāṇḍavas (MBh).

ध्येय (*dhyeya*) M. "worth meditating on", Hanumān (HS). **ध्येया** (*dhyeyā*) F. Rādhā (RKS), Gaṅgā (GS3).

ध्रौव्या (*dhrauvyā*) F. "firm, constant, unwavering", Yamunā (YS). **ध्रौव्य** (*dhrauvya*) M.

नन्दजा (*nandajā*) F. "born from bliss", Gāyatrī (GS4). **नन्दज** (*nandaja*) M.

नन्देन्दु (*nandendu*) MF. "the pleasant moon, the moon among those who rejoice", a king (VāP).

नभस्य (*nabhasya*) M. "skilled in [matters of] the sky", son of Svārociṣa Manu (MaP). **नभस्या** (*nabhasyā*) F.

नभस्वान् (*nabhasvān*) M. "related to the sky, young", Sūrya (SS1). **नभस्वती** (*nabhasvatī*) F. a queen (BhP).

नमस्कार्या (*namaskāryā*) F. "worth worshipping or venerating", Gaṅgā (GS3). **नमस्कार्य** (*namaskārya*) M.

नमस्या (*namasyā*) F. "venerable, respectable", Durgā (DS3). **नमस्य** (*namasya*) M.

नमस्यु (*namasyu*) MF. "saluting, bowing down", a king (BhP).

नरिष्यन्त (*nariṣyanta*) M. "not hurting or killing, non-violent", son of Vaivasvata Manu (BhP).

नवरथ (*navaratha*) M. "he whose chariots are new", a king (BhP). **नवरथा** (*navarathā*) F.

नवाक्ष (*navākṣa*) M. "with new (=beautiful) eyes", a *vānara* (BrP). **नवाक्षी** (*navākṣī*) F.

नादाख्या (*nādākhyā*) F. "she whose appellation is *nāda*", Sītā (SS2). **नादाख्य** (*nādākhya*) M.

नादेशी (*nādeśī*) F. "the goddess of *nāda* (sound or resonance)", Rādhā (RS2). **नादेश** (*nādeśa*) M.

नायिका (*nāyikā*) F. "she who leads, a female leader", Rādhā (RS2). **नायक** (*nāyaka*) M.

नारदी (*nāradī*) F. "associated with Nārada, belonging to Nārada", Yamunā (YS). **नारद** (*nārada*) M.

निग्रह (*nigraha*) M. "subduing or controlling [everybody]", Viṣṇu (VS1), Śiva (ŚS1). **निग्रहा** (*nigrahā*) F.

निघ्न (*nighna*) M. "obedient", a king (BrP). **निघ्ना** (*nighnā*) F.

नित्याङ्गी (*nityāṅgī*) F. "with an imperishable form", Rādhā (RS2). **नित्याङ्ग** (*nityāṅga*) M.

निदाघ (*nidāgha*) M. "he who burns down [ignorance]", son of Brahmā (VāP). **निदाघा** (*nidāghā*) F.

निधिदा (*nidhidā*) F. "bestower of treasures", Annapūrṇā (AS), Gāyatrī (GS4). **निधिद** (*nidhida*) M.

निध्रुव (*nidhruva*) M. "completely firm or stable, eternal", a *ṛṣi* (BrP, VāP). **निध्रुवा** (*nidhruvā*) F.

निमेषिणी (*nimeṣiṇī*) F. "with [beautiful] blinking of eyes", Gāyatrī (GS4). **निमेषी** (*nimeṣī*) M.

नियता (*niyatā*) F. "self-restrained", Gaṅgā (GS3). **नियत** (*niyata*) M.

नियन्त्रा (*niyantrā*) F. "she who restrains or controls", Lakṣmī (LS2). **नियन्त्र** (*niyantra*) M.

नियामक (*niyāmaka*) M. "he who restrains or controls", Narasiṃha (NS). **नियामिका** (*niyāmikā*) F.

नियुत्सा (*niyutsā*) F. "extremely willing to fight, a female warrior", a queen (BhP). **नियुत्स** (*niyutsa*) M.

निरत्रप (*niratrapa*) M. "modest, humble", Hanumān (HS). **निरत्रपा** (*niratrapā*) F.

निरन्तरा (*nirantarā*) F. "unbounded, uninterrupted", Rādhā (RS2), Lalitā (LS1). **निरन्तर** (*nirantara*) M. Dattātreya (DS2).

निरमित्र (*niramitra*) M. "free from enemies", son of Nakula (MBh). **निरमित्रा** (*niramitrā*) F.

निरवद्या (*niravadyā*) F. "blameless, irreproachable", Gāyatrī (GS4), Lalitā (LS1). **निरवद्य** (*niravadya*) M. Kṛṣṇa (KS1), Narasiṃha (NS).

निराकुल (*nirākula*) M. "calm, tranquil, not perplexed", Sūrya (SS1). **निराकुला** (*nirākulā*) F. Rādhā (RS2).

निराम (*nirāma*) M. "he in whom *yogīs* rejoice completely or forever", Śiva (ŚS5). **निरामा** (*nirāmā*) F.

निरामया (*nirāmayā*) F. "without [physical and mental] diseases", Lakṣmī (LS2), Sītā (SS2), Rādhā (RS2), Lalitā (LS1). **निरामय** (*nirāmaya*) M.

निरायुध (*nirāyudha*) M. "without any arms or weapons", Dattātreya (DS2). **निरायुधा** (*nirāyudhā*) F.

निरालम्ब (*nirālamba*) M. "not dependent on anything or anybody", Narasiṃha (NS). **निरालम्बा** (*nirālambā*) F. Lalitā (LS1).

निरालोका (*nirālokā*) F. "having come from light", Rādhā (RS2). **निरालोक** (*nirāloka*) M.

निरासक्त (*nirāsakta*) M. "free from attachment", Dattātreya (DS2). **निरासक्ता** (*nirāsaktā*) F.

निरीहा (*nirīhā*) F. "without desires", Gaṅgā (GS3), Bhavānī (BS). **निरीह** (*nirīha*) M. Rāma (RS1).

निरुक्त (*nirukta*) M. "expressed or explained [by scriptures]", Kṛṣṇa (KS1), Narasiṃha (NS). **निरुक्ता** (*niruktā*) F.

निरुत्सुक (*nirutsuka*) M. "not anxious, calm", son of Raivata Manu (MaP). **निरुत्सुका** (*nirutsukā*) F.

निर्गता (*nirgatā*) F. "she who appeared [from the waters], manifest", Lakṣmī (LS2). **निर्गत** (*nirgata*) M.

निर्गुणा (*nirguṇā*) F. "beyond qualities, without [bad] qualities [which are worth abandoning]", Gāyatrī (GS4). **निर्गुण** (*nirguṇa*) M.

निर्द्वैता (*nirdvaitā*) F. "free from duality", Lalitā (LS1). **निर्द्वैत** (*nirdvaita*) M.

निर्नाशा (*nirnāśā*) F. "imperishable, eternal", Lalitā (LS1). **निर्नाश** (*nirnāśa*) M.

निर्भवा (*nirbhavā*) F. "without an origin, unborn, uncreated", Lalitā (LS1). **निर्भव** (*nirbhava*) M.

निर्भेदा (*nirbhedā*) F. "she who is without any *bheda* (difference)", Lalitā (LS1). **निर्भेद** (*nirbheda*) M.

निर्मदा (*nirmadā*) F. "humble, without pride or arrogance", Lalitā (LS1). **निर्मद** (*nirmada*) M. Śiva (ŚS3).

निर्ममा (*nirmamā*) F. "not selfish, indifferent", Lalitā (LS1). **निर्मम** (*nirmama*) M. Viṣṇu (VS2).

निर्मोक (*nirmoka*) M. "he who liberates, setting free", son of Sāvarṇi Manu (BhP). **निर्मोका** (*nirmokā*) F.

निर्मोहा (*nirmohā*) F. "she who is without *moha* (illusion or ignorance)", Lalitā (LS1). **निर्मोह** (*nirmoha*) M. Narasiṃha (NS), son of Raivata Manu (MaP).

निर्लेपा (*nirlepā*) F. "she who is without the *lepa* or bondage of karma", Gaṅgā (GS3), Lalitā (LS1). **निर्लेप** (*nirlepa*) M.

निर्लोभा (*nirlobhā*) F. "she who is without greed", Lalitā (LS1). **निर्लोभ** (*nirlobha*) M.

निर्विकल्प (*nirvikalpa*) M. "free from doubts, without any alternative", Hanumān (HS). **निर्विकल्पा** (*nirvikalpā*) F.

निर्विशेषा (*nirviśeṣā*) F. "she who is without any qualities (=absolute), the supreme Brahman", Bhavānī (BS). **निर्विशेष** (*nirviśeṣa*) M.

निर्वैरा (*nirvairā*) F. "without enmity", Annapūrṇā (AS), Bhavānī (BS). **निर्वैर** (*nirvaira*) M.

निर्व्योमा (*nirvyomā*) F. "she who came forth from *vyoman* (=water or the ocean)", Lakṣmī (LS2). **निर्व्योम** (*nirvyoma*) M.

निशालय (*niśālaya*) M. "he in whom the night (=ignorance) dissolves", Śiva (ŚS1). **निशालया** (*niśālayā*) F.

निश्चर (*niścara*) M. "unshakeable, immovable", a *ṛṣi* (BrP). **निश्चरा** (*niścarā*) F.

निश्चिन्ता (*niścintā*) F. "free from worry or anxiety", Lalitā (LS1). **निश्चिन्त** (*niścinta*) M.

निष्कम्पा (*niṣkampā*) F. "unshakeable, not trembling or moving", Lakṣmī (LS2). **निष्कम्प** (*niṣkampa*) M.

निष्कामा (*niṣkāmā*) F. "without [mundane or selfish] desires, unselfish", Lalitā (LS1). **निष्काम** (*niṣkāma*) M.

निष्क्रोधा (*niṣkrodhā*) F. "free from anger", Lalitā (LS1). **निष्क्रोध** (*niṣkrodha*) M.

निष्पापा (*niṣpāpā*) F. "free from *pāpa*", Lalitā (LS1). **निष्पाप** (*niṣpāpa*) M.

निस्तुला (*nistulā*) F. "incomparable, unrivalled, without a parallel", Lalitā (LS1). **निस्तुल** (*nistula*) M.

नीतिदा (*nītidā*) F. "bestower of prudence or wisdom", Annapūrṇā (AS). **नीतिद** (*nītida*) M.

नीरागा (*nīrāgā*) F. "without [mortal] attachment or passion", Lalitā (LS1). **नीराग** (*nīrāga*) M.

नीरुजा (*nīrujā*) F. "free from illness, healthy", Yamunā (YS). **नीरुज** (*nīruja*) M.

नीलाभा (*nīlābhā*) F. "blue-hued, with a bluish splendour", Yamunā (YS). **नीलाभ** (*nīlābha*) M.

नृपञ्जय (*nṛpañjaya*) M. "conqueror of kings", a king (BhP). **नृपञ्जया** (*nṛpañjayā*) F.

नैगमेय (*naigameya*) M. "devoted to *nigama* (Vedas)", an *aṃśa* of Skanda (BrP, VāP, ViP). **नैगमेयी** (*naigameyī*) F.

नैध्रुव (*naidhruva*) M. "completely firm or stable", a *ṛṣi* (BrP, MaP). **नैध्रुवी** (*naidhruvī*) F.

नैमिषी (*naimiṣī*) F. "associated with Naimiṣāraṇya", Yamunā (YS). **नैमिष** (*naimiṣa*) M.

नैष्कर्म्या (*naiṣkarmyā*) F. "without the bondage of *karma*", Lalitā (LS1). **नैष्कर्म्य** (*naiṣkarmya*) M.

नोदिता (*noditā*) F. "she who is impelled, inspired", used for divine speech (KYM). **नोदित** (*nodita*) M.

पञ्चाङ्गी (*pañcāṅgī*) F. "having five limbs (e.g. five parts of a *pañcāṅga*)", Gāyatrī (GS4). **पञ्चाङ्ग** (*pañcāṅga*) M.

पञ्चिका (*pañcikā*) F. "associated with five [elements]", Gāyatrī (GS4). **पञ्चक** (*pañcaka*) M.

पथिका (*pathikā*) F. "a guide, a traveller", Gāyatrī (GS4). **पथिक** (*pathika*) M.

पथ्या (*pathyā*) F. "suitable, proper, the path [to *mokṣa*]", Gaṅgā (GS3). **पथ्य** (*pathya*) M.

पद्मस्था (*padmasthā*) F. "situated in the lotus", Annapūrṇā (AS), Lakṣmī (LS2). **पद्मस्थ** (*padmastha*) M.

पद्माक्ष (*padmākṣa*) M. "lotus-eyed", Kṛṣṇa (RKS). **पद्माक्षी**

(*padmākṣī*) F.

पद्माङ्का (*padmāṅkā*) F. "she whose mark or sign is the lotus", Lakṣmī (LS2). **पद्माङ्क** (*padmāṅka*) M.

पद्माभ (*padmābha*) M. "having the beauty of a lotus", Narasiṃha (NS). **पद्माभा** (*padmābhā*) F.

पद्मास्या (*padmāsyā*) F. "she whose face is beautiful like the lotus", Annapūrṇā (AS). **पद्मास्य** (*padmāsya*) M.

पनस्यु (*panasyu*) MF. "worthy of praise", used for Indra and Maruts (ṚVŚ).

पयस्विनी (*payasvinī*) F. "she whose water is praiseworthy", Gaṅgā (GS3).

परमिका (*paramikā*) F. "best, most excellent, greatest, principal, first", used to describe Daśaratha's affection for Rāma (VR). **परमक** (*paramaka*) M.

परमेषु (*parameṣu*) MF. "with excellent arrows", a king (MaP).

पराक्ष (*parākṣa*) M. "having the best eyes (*ākṣis*), he whose senses (*ākṣas*) are [fixed] on *para* (Brahman)", a king (BrP). **पराक्षी/पराक्षा** (*parākṣī/parākṣā*) F. Note: **पराक्षी** (*parākṣī*) means "she who has the the best eyes (*akṣis*)" while **पराक्षा** (*parākṣā*) means "she whose senses (*ākṣas*) are [fixed] on *para* (Brahman)".

पराङ्कुशा (*parāṅkuśā*) F. "she who controls *paras* (enemies)", Lalitā (BrP). **पराङ्कुश** (*parāṅkuśa*) M.

पराद्या (*parādyā*) F. "supreme and eternal", used for Rādhā (BVP). **पराद्य** (*parādya*) M.

पराधीश (*parādhīśa*) M. "the supreme emperor or lord", Kṛṣṇa (RKS). **पराधीशा** (*parādhīśā*) F.

परानन्द (*parānanda*) M. "he whose bliss is supreme", Viṣṇu (VS2). **परानन्दा** (*parānandā*) F.

पराम्बिका (*parāmbikā*) F. "the supreme mother", Gāyatrī (GS4), a *śakti* (BrP).

परार्ध (*parārdha*) M. "the most excellent", Viṣṇu (VS2), the greatest number (one hundred quadrillion) in ŚYM. **परार्धा** (*parārdhā*) F.

परावसु (*parāvasu*) MF. "one who stays away from riches", a *ṛṣi* (MBh).

परिघ (*parigha*) M. "the destroyer [of enemies]", a king (MaP). **परिघा** (*parighā*) F.

परेशी (*pareśī*) F. "the supreme goddess", Annapūrṇā (AS). **परेश** (*pareśa*) M.

परोदय (*parodaya*) M. "the source of supreme exaltation or ascent", Viṣṇu (VS2). **परोदया** (*parodayā*) F.

पर्णिनी (*parṇinī*) F. "having leaves [for worship]", an Apsaras (BrP, VāP). **पर्णी** (*parṇī*) M.

पर्यय (*paryaya*) M. "pervading [everything] from all sides", Śiva (ŚS1). **पर्यया** (*paryayā*) F.

पाराशर्य (*pārāśarya*) M. "descendant of Parāśara", Vyāsa (MBh). **पाराशरी** (*pārāśarī*) F.

पार्थध्वज (*pārthadhvaja*) M. "[situated on] the banner of Arjuna", Hanumān (HS).

पार्थिवा (*pārthivā*) F. "daughter of the earth", Lakṣmī (LS3). **पार्थिव** (*pārthiva*) M.

पार्षदा (*pārṣadā*) F. "skilled in an assembly, a companion or attendant [of Kṛṣṇa]", Yamunā (YS). **पार्षद** (*pārṣada*) M.

पालिनी (*pālinī*) F. "she who protects or nourishes", Gaṅgā (GS3). **पाली** (*pālī*) M. son of Pṛthu (VāP).

पावक (*pāvaka*) M. "he who purifies", Agni (MBh). **पाविका** (*pāvikā*) F.

पाविनी (*pāvinī*) F. "she who purifies", Gāyatrī (GS4). **पावी** (*pāvī*) M.

पिङ्गला (*piṅgalā*) F. "yellowish", *piṅgalā nāḍī*, Lakṣmī (LS2). **पिङ्गल** (*piṅgala*) M.

पिङ्गाक्ष (*piṅgākṣa*) M. "with reddish-brown eyes", Narasiṃha (NS), Hanumān (HS). **पिङ्गाक्षी** (*piṅgākṣī*) F.

पुण्यश्लोक (*puṇyaśloka*) M. "he whose *śloka* (fame) is good or auspicious", Hanumān (HS), Yudhiṣṭhira (BhP). **पुण्यश्लोका** (*puṇyaślokā*) F.

पुण्याङ्गी (*puṇyāṅgī*) F. "having virtuous or beautiful limbs or body", Yamunā (YS). **पुण्याङ्ग** (*puṇyāṅga*) M.

पुण्येयु (*puṇyeyu*) MF. "desirous of merit", a king (MaP).

पुरजित् (*purajit*) MF. "conqueror of [the three] *puras* (cities)", Śiva (ŚS2).

पुरन्ध्री (*purandhrī*) F. "she who bears or supports the *pura* (household or city)", Gāyatrī (GS4).

पुरातन (*purātana*) M. "ancient, primeval", Śiva (ŚS3). **पुरातनी** (*purātanī*) F.

पुरुहूत (*puruhūta*) M. "invoked (=worshipped) by many", Indra (AK). **पुरुहूता** (*puruhūtā*) F. a *devī* (MaP).

पुरुहोत्र (*puruhotra*) M. "he who has many offerings [for Agni], he who performs many *yajñas*", a king (BhP). **पुरुहोत्रा** (*puruhotrā*) F.

पुरोजव (*purojava*) M. "possessing great speed, swift", a king (BhP). **पुरोजवा** (*purojavā*) F.

पुलस्त्य (*pulastya*) M. "he whose sound (=word) reaches far and wide", a *ṛṣi* (MBh). **पुलस्त्या** (*pulastyā*) F.

पुलह (*pulaha*) M. "going far and wide", a *ṛṣi* (MBh). **पुलहा** (*pulahā*) F.

पुष्करा (*puṣkarā*) F. "the giver of nourishment", Lalitā (LS1). **पुष्कर** (*puṣkara*) M.

पुष्कराक्ष (*puṣkarākṣa*) M. "lotus-eyed", Viṣṇu (VS1), Narasiṃha (NS). **पुष्कराक्षी** (*puṣkarākṣī*) F.

पुष्करिणी (*puṣkariṇī*) F. "with many lotuses, an excellent woman", a queen (BhP). **पुष्करी** (*puṣkarī*) M.

पुष्टिदा (*puṣṭidā*) F. "she who bestows nourishment or prosperity", Gāyatrī (GS4), Bhavānī (BS). **पुष्टिद** (*puṣṭida*) M.

पुष्पवान् (*puṣpavān*) M. "rich in flowers or politeness", a king (BhP). **पुष्पवती** (*puṣpavatī*) F.

पूरिका (*pūrikā*) F. "she who completes, she who is complete", name of a city (BrP). **पूरक** (*pūraka*) M.

पूर्णाशा (*pūrṇāśā*) F. "with all desires fulfilled, fulfilling desires", Gāyatrī (GS4). **पूर्णाश** (*pūrṇāśa*) M.

पूर्वचित्ति (*pūrvacitti*) MF. "one whose thought is before [their action]", an Apsaras (BhP).

पृथुञ्जय/पृथुजय (*pṛthuñjaya/pṛthujaya*) M. "conquering the greats", a king (ViP, BrP). **पृथुञ्जया/पृथुजया** (*pṛthuñjayā/pṛthujayā*) F.

पृथुलाक्ष (*pṛthulākṣa*) M. "having large eyes", a king (BhP). **पृथुलाक्षी** (*pṛthulākṣī*) F.

पृथुसेन (*pṛthusena*) M. "he who has a large army", a king (BhP). **पृथुसेना** (*pṛthusenā*) F.

पृश्नि (*pṛśni*) MF. "thin, delicate, slender", a *ṛṣi* (MBh), Devakī in a previous birth (BhP).

पोषणी (*poṣaṇī*) F. "nourishing, supporting", Sītā (SS2). **पोषण** (*poṣaṇa*) M.

पोषिणी (*poṣiṇī*) F. "she who nourishes or protects", Bhavānī

(BS). **पोषी** (*poṣī*) M.

प्रकाशक (*prakāśaka*) M. "illuminating, brilliant, resplendent", Sūrya (SS1). **प्रकाशिका** (*prakāśikā*) F.

प्रग्रह (*pragraha*) M. "accepting [the offerings of *bhaktas*]", Viṣṇu (VS1). **प्रग्रहा** (*pragrahā*) F.

प्रघोष (*praghoṣa*) M. "with an eminent sound or roar", son of Kṛṣṇa (BhP). **प्रघोषा** (*praghoṣā*) F.

प्रचेतना (*pracetanā*) F. "illuminating, enlightening", Yamunā (YS). **प्रचेतन** (*pracetana*) M.

प्रचेतस् (*pracetas*) MF. "with an eminent mind, wise", a *ṛṣi* (MBh).

प्रजवी (*prajavī*) M. "quick, swift, speedy", used for Lakṣmaṇa (BK). **प्रजविनी** (*prajavinī*) F.

प्रजागर (*prajāgara*) M. "eminently awake, ever-conscious", Viṣṇu (VS1), Rāma (RS1). **प्रजागरा** (*prajāgarā*) F.

प्रणवेशी (*praṇaveśī*) F. "the goddess in *praṇava* (OM)", Rādhā (RS2). **प्रणवेश** (*praṇaveśa*) M.

प्रतप्त (*pratapta*) M. "having performed askesis,", Rāma (RS1). **प्रतप्ता** (*prataptā*) F.

प्रतर्दन (*pratardana*) M. "he who pierces/destroys [darkness]", Viṣṇu (VS1), Sūrya (SS1). **प्रतर्दनी** (*pratardanī*) F.

प्रतापन (*pratāpana*) M. "very hot, excessively heating", Viṣṇu (VS1), Sūrya (SS1). **प्रतापनी** (*pratāpanī*) F.

प्रतापवान् (*pratāpavān*) M. "possessing brilliance or power", Kṛṣṇa (KS2). **प्रतापवती** (*pratāpavatī*) F.

प्रत्यग्र (*pratyagra*) M. "new, young, fresh", Hanumān (HS), a king (BhP). **प्रत्यग्रा** (*pratyagrā*) F.

प्रत्यङ्गिरस् (*pratyaṅgiras*) MF. "one who advances", Lakṣmī (LS2).

प्रद्योतन (*pradyotana*) M. "eminently brillant, shining", Sūrya (SS1). **प्रद्योतनी** (*pradyotanī*) F.

प्रधानेशी (*pradhāneśī*) F. "the goddess of the best ones", Lalitā (BrP). **प्रधानेश** (*pradhāneśa*) M.

प्रबला (*prabalā*) F. "eminently powerful, very strong or intense", Durgā (DS3). **प्रबल** (*prabala*) M.

प्रभविष्णु (*prabhaviṣṇu*) MF. "mighty, distinguished", Rāma (RS1), Kṛṣṇa (KS1), Narasiṃha (NS), Dattātreya (DS2).

प्रभामय (*prabhāmaya*) M. "full of dazzling brilliance", Sūrya (SS1). **प्रभामयी** (*prabhāmayī*) F.

प्रभावा (*prabhāvā*) F. "with eminent properties or qualities", Lakṣmī (LS2). **प्रभाव** (*prabhāva*) M.

प्रभावान् (*prabhāvān*) M. "shining, radiant, splendid", Sūrya (SS1). **प्रभावती** (*prabhāvatī*) F.

प्रभासेश (*prabhāseśa*) M. "the god of splendour", Śiva (VāP). **प्रभासेशी** (*prabhāseśī*) F.

प्रभूष्णु (*prabhūṣṇu*) MF. "powerful, strong, capable", Kṛṣṇa

(KS1).

प्रमति (*pramati*) MF. "having an eminent intellect", a king (BhP).

प्रमन्थु (*pramanthu*) MF. "an eminent thinker", a king (BhP).

प्रमर्दन (*pramardana*) M. "he who crushes [his enemies]", a *vānara* (BrP). **प्रमर्दनी** (*pramardanī*) F.

प्रमोदन (*pramodana*) M. "gladdening, pleasing, delighting", Viṣṇu (VS1). **प्रमोदनी** (*pramodanī*) F.

प्ररोहा (*prarohā*) F. "growing forth", Lakṣmī (LS2). **प्ररोह** (*praroha*) M.

प्रलम्ब (*pralamba*) M. "prominent", Kṛṣṇa (KS1). **प्रलम्बा** (*pralambā*) F.

प्रवर्तन (*pravartana*) M. "he who inspires or prompts to action", Dattātreya (DS2). **प्रवर्तनी** (*pravartanī*) F.

प्रशस्ता (*praśastā*) F. "praised, commendable, excellent, auspicious". **प्रशस्त** (*praśasta*) M.

प्रश्रय (*praśraya*) M. "having respect and affection", son of Dharma (BhP). **प्रश्रया** (*praśrayā*) F.

प्रसवा (*prasavā*) F. "with eminent progeny, giving birth", Gāyatrī (GS4).

प्रसवित्री (*prasavitrī*) F. "she who gives birth [to the universe]", Lalitā (LS1). **प्रसविता** (*prasavitā*) M.

प्रसहन (*prasahana*) M. "eminently enduring or patient", Gaṇeśa (GS2). **प्रसहना** (*prasahanā*) F.

प्रस्कण्व (*praskaṇva*) M. "very praiseworthy or honourable, he whose praisers are eminent", a *ṛṣi* (ṚVŚ).

प्रस्कन्दन (*praskandana*) M. "he who causes [even the immovable] to move", Śiva (ŚS1). **प्रस्कन्दनी** (*praskandanī*) F.

प्रस्तुत (*prastuta*) M. "eminently praised or eulogized", Narasiṃha (NS). **प्रस्तुता** (*prastutā*) F.

प्रहर्षण (*praharṣaṇa*) M. "he who gladdens or delights", Kṛṣṇa (KS1). **प्रहर्षणी** (*praharṣaṇī*) F.

प्रहस (*prahasa*) M. "he whose laughter is eminent", Śiva (ŚS5). **प्रहसा** (*prahasā*) F.

प्रहास (*prahāsa*) M. "he whose laughter is eminent", Śiva (TK). **प्रहासा** (*prahāsā*) F.

प्रह्वा (*prahvā*) F. "humble, modest", Lakṣmī (LS2). **प्रह्व** (*prahva*) M.

प्राणदा (*prāṇadā*) F. "the giver of *prāṇas* (life)", Lakṣmī (LS2). **प्राणद** (*prāṇada*) M.

प्राणेशी (*prāṇeśī*) F. "the goddess of *prāṇas*", Gaṅgā (GS3). **प्राणेश** (*prāṇeśa*) M.

प्रापणी (*prāpaṇī*) F. "she who makes [devotees] attain [mokṣa]", Lakṣmī (LS2). **प्रापण** (*prāpaṇa*) M.

प्रियश्रवस् (*priyaśravas*) MF. "one whose glory is pleasant [to hear]", used for Viṣṇu (BhP).

प्रोज्ज्वला (*projjvalā*) F. "eminently brilliant or beautiful", Yamunā (YS). **प्रोज्ज्वल** (*projjvala*) M.

प्रोन्नता (*pronnatā*) F. "lofty, superior, strong", Yamunā (YS). **प्रोन्नत** (*pronnata*) M.

प्रोष्या (*proṣyā*) F. "wandering, roaming", Yamunā (YS). **प्रोष्य** (*proṣya*) M.

फलदा (*phaladā*) F. "the bestower of fruits [of *karma*]", Gāyatrī (GS4). **फलद** (*phalada*) M.

फलिनी (*phalinī*) F. "fruitful, yielding fruits, having an advantage", Gāyatrī (GS4), Gaṅgā (GS3). **फली** (*phalī*) M.

बर्हिषद् (*barhiṣad*) MF. "seated on the *barhi* grass [for performing a *yajña*)", a king (BhP).

बर्हिष्मती (*barhiṣmatī*) F. "she who worships, brilliant, shining", Yamunā (YS). **बर्हिष्मान्** (*barhiṣmān*) M.

बलानुज (*balānuja*) M. "younger brother of Balarāma", Kṛṣṇa (RKS). **बलानुजा** (*balānujā*) F. "younger sister of Balarāma", Subhadrā (referred to as *anujāṃ vāsudevasya* in MBh).

बहुदा (*bahudā*) F. "bestowing a lot", Yamunā (YS). **बहुद** (*bahuda*) M.

बहुरथ (*bahuratha*) M. "having many chariots", a king (BhP). **बहुरथा** (*bahurathā*) F.

बहुविद्य (*bahuvidya*) M. "very learned", Śiva (ŚS1). **बहुविद्या**

(*bahuvidyā*) F.

बहुश्रुत (*bahuśruta*) M. "he who has heard (=learned) a lot, learned, the source of many scriptures (*śāstras*)", Śiva (ŚS3). **बहुश्रुता** (*bahuśrutā*) F.

बह्वृच (*bahvṛca*) M. "possessing (knowing) many *ṛcs* (mantras of Ṛgveda)", a *ṛṣi* (BrP). **बह्वृची** (*bahvṛcī*) F.

बादरायण (*bādarāyaṇa*) M. "dwelling in *badarikāśrama*", Vyāsa (BhP). **बादरायणी** (*bādarāyaṇī*) F.

बीभत्सु (*bībhatsu*) MF. "abhorring [that which is abhorrent]", Arjuna (MBh).

बुद्धिदा (*buddhidā*) F. "the bestower of intellect", Bhavānī (BS). **बुद्धिद** (*buddhida*) M.

बृहती (*bṛhatī*) F. "expansive, great, strong, powerful, bright, clear", Gāyatrī (GS4), Sītā (SS2), Lalitā (LS1). **बृहन्** (*bṛhan*) M.

बृहत्कर्मा (*bṛhatkarmā*) MF. "one with great or mighty acts", a king (BrP).

बृहत्सेन (*bṛhatsena*) M. "he who has a strong army", a king (MBh). **बृहत्सेना** (*bṛhatsenā*) F.

बृहदिषु (*bṛhadiṣu*) MF. "one with powerful arrows", a king (BhP).

बृहदीश (*bṛhadīśa*) M. "the great lord", similar to name *bṛhadīśvara* of Hanumān (HS). **बृहदीशी** (*bṛhadīśī*) F.

बृहद्भानु (*bṛhadbhānu*) MF. "with many rays of light, very bright", Dattātreya (DS2).

बृहद्यशस् (*bṛhadyaśas*) MF. "he whose fame is far-reaching", son of Sāvarṇi Manu (BrP).

बृहन्त (*bṛhanta*) M. "great, strong, bright", a king (BhP). **बृहन्ती** (*bṛhantī*) F.

बोधिता (*bodhitā*) F. "enlightened, instructed", Gāyatrī (GS4). **बोधित** (*bodhita*) M.

बोध्य (*bodhya*) M. "worth knowing or understanding", disciple of Bāṣkala (BrP). **बोध्या** (*bodhyā*) F.

बौधेय (*baudheya*) M. "intelligent, wise", disciple of Yājñavalkya (BrP). **बौधेयी** (*baudheyī*) F.

ब्रह्मण्य (*brahmaṇya*) M. "beneficial for or well-disposed towards *brahman* (askesis, Vedas, truth, Brāhmaṇas, and knowledge)", Viṣṇu (VS1), Rāma (RS1), Narasiṃha (NS), Kṛṣṇa (KS2), Gaṇeśa (GS2). **ब्रह्मण्या** (*brahmaṇyā*) F. Gaṅgā (GS3).

ब्रह्मदा (*brahmadā*) F. "she who bestows *brahman* (askesis, Vedas, truth, and knowledge)", a river (VāP). **ब्रह्मद** (*brahmada*) M.

ब्रह्ममय (*brahmamaya*) M. "consisting of *brahman* (Vedas, askesis, or Brahman)", Kṛṣṇa (KS1). **ब्रह्ममयी** (*brahmamayī*) F.

ब्रह्मवित्/ब्रह्मविद् (*brahmavit/brahmavid*) MF. "one who knows *brahman*", Viṣṇu (VS1), Śiva (ŚS1).

ब्रह्मिष्ठा (*brahmiṣṭhā*) F. "the best among the knowers of *brahman* (=Vedas)", Lakṣmī (LS2). **ब्रह्मिष्ठ** (*brahmiṣṭha*) M.

ब्रह्मेशी (*brahmeśī*) F. "the goddess of *brahman* (Vedas)", Annapūrṇā (AS). **ब्रह्मेश** (*brahmeśa*) M.

ब्रह्मेषु (*brahmeṣu*) MF. "having arrows of *brahman* (truth)", a king (VāP).

भजमान (*bhajamāna*) M. "serving, worshipping, right, proper", a king (BhP). **भजमाना** (*bhajamānā*) F.

भज्य (*bhajya*) M. "worthy of being served", disciple of Bāṣkali (BhP). **भज्या** (*bhajyā*) F.

भद्रदा (*bhadradā*) F. "bestower of auspiciousness", Gāyatrī (GS4). **भद्रद** (*bhadrada*) M.

भद्रदेव (*bhadradeva*) M. "the auspicious *deva* (god)", son of Devakī and Vasudeva (BrP). **भद्रदेवी** (*bhadradevī*) F.

भद्रवती (*bhadravatī*) F. "possessing auspiciousness, bliss, or prosperity", daughter of Kṛṣṇa (BrP). **भद्रवान्** (*bhadravān*) M.

भयासख (*bhayāsakha*) M. "enemy of fear, unafraid", son of Vasudeva (VāP). **भयासखा** (*bhayāsakhā*) F.

भर्ग (*bharga*) M. "having light or lustre", Sūrya (SS1), Rāma (RS1), Hanumān (HS). **भर्गा** (*bhargā*) F.

भविष्णु (*bhaviṣṇu*) MF. "thriving, existing well", Narasiṃha (NS), Hanumān (HS).

भवेशी (*bhaveśī*) F. "goddess of the world", Annapūrṇā (AS). **भवेश** (*bhaveśa*) M.

भागन्य (*bhāganya*) M. "possessing fortune, fortunate", a *rājarṣi* (VāP). **भागन्या** (*bhāganyā*) F.

भागिल (*bhāgila*) M. "fortunate", a *pravara* (MaP). **भागिला** (*bhāgilā*) F.

भानुमान् (*bhānumān*) M. "possessing light, luminous, brilliant", Sūrya (SS1). **भानुमती** (*bhānumatī*) F.

भामक (*bhāmaka*) M. "raging [in battle or against the evil ones]", Kṛṣṇa (KS2). **भामिका** (*bhāmikā*) F.

भार्गवेश (*bhārgaveśa*) M. "lord of the Bhārgavas (Paraśurāma)", name of *kṣetra* (MaP). **भार्गवेशी** (*bhārgaveśī*) F.

भावग (*bhāvaga*) M. "he who follows (=understands) feelings [of devotees]", Hanumān (HS). **भावगा** (*bhāvagā*) F.

भाषी (*bhāṣī*) F. "she who speaks [well]", a queen (VāP). **भाष** (*bhāṣa*) M.

भासक (*bhāsaka*) M. "enlightening, illuminating", Narasiṃha (NS). **भासिका** (*bhāsikā*) F.

भासन (*bhāsana*) M. "shining, illuminating", Sūrya (SS1). **भासनी** (*bhāsanī*) F.

भासित (*bhāsita*) M. "brilliant, radiant, shining", Sūrya (SS1). **भासिता** (*bhāsitā*) F.

भासुरा (*bhāsurā*) F. "shining, brilliant, resplendent", Lakṣmī

(LS2). भासुर (*bhāsura*) M. a *deva* (BrP).

भासुरी (*bhāsurī*) F. "shining, brilliant, resplendent", Lakṣmī (LS2). भासुर (*bhāsura*) M.

भास्करी (*bhāskarī*) F. "shining, resplendent", Lakṣmī (LS2). भास्कर (*bhāskara*) M.

भास्वरा (*bhāsvarā*) F. "radiant, brilliant, shining", Lakṣmī (LS2), Annapūrṇā (AS). भास्वर (*bhāsvara*) M.

भास्वान् (*bhāsvān*) M. "luminous, splendid, shining", Hanumān (HS). भास्वती (*bhāsvatī*) F. Annapūrṇā (AS).

भिषक् (*bhiṣak*) MF. "healer, physician", Viṣṇu (VS1).

भीमाक्षी (*bhīmākṣī*) F. "with terrifying eyes", Annapūrṇā (AS). भीमाक्ष (*bhīmākṣa*) M.

भुवमन्यु (*bhuvamanyu*) MF. "one whose rage [in a battle] is like the fire", a king (MaP).

भुवस्पति (*bhuvaspati*) M. "the lord of the *bhuvar-loka*", Vāyu (BrP, VāP).

भूगर्भ (*bhūgarbha*) M. "with the earth in his belly", Viṣṇu (VS1). भूगर्भा (*bhūgarbhā*) F.

भूतिदा (*bhūtidā*) F. "she who bestows welfare or prosperity", Gaṅgā (GS3), Gāyatrī (GS4). भूतिद (*bhūtida*) M.

भूमा (*bhūmā*) MF. "great, large, having a lot", a king (BhP).

भूरिदा (*bhūridā*) F. "she who gives a lot, munificent", Gaṅgā

(GS3). **भूरिद** (*bhūrida*) M.

भूष्णु (*bhūṣṇu*) MF. "existing [well], desiring prosperity", Sūrya (SS1).

भूष्य (*bhūṣya*) M. "worthy of being adorned", Sūrya (SS1). **भूष्या** (*bhūṣyā*) F.

भैरवेश (*bhairaveśa*) M. "the god of *bhairavas*", Viṣṇu (VS2). **भैरवेशी** (*bhairaveśī*) F.

भ्राजित (*bhrājita*) M. "brilliant, radiant, shining", a group of *devas* (ViP). **भ्राजिता** (*bhrājitā*) F.

भ्राजिष्ठ (*bhrājiṣṭha*) M. "most resplendent, very bright", a king (BhP). **भ्राजिष्ठा** (*bhrājiṣṭhā*) F.

भ्राजिष्णु (*bhrājiṣṇu*) MF. "shining, brilliant", Viṣṇu (VS1), Rāma (RS1), Narasiṃha (NS), Hanumān (HS).

मतिदा (*matidā*) F. "she who grants intellect", Gaṅgā (GS3). **मतिद** (*matida*) M.

मदनेश (*madaneśa*) M. "the lord of *madana* (Kāmadeva)", Kṛṣṇa (RKS). **मदनेशी** (*madaneśī*) F.

मदापह (*madāpaha*) M. "the slayer of arrogance", Dattātreya (DS2). **मदापहा** (*madāpahā*) F.

मदालसा (*madālasā*) F. "inactive in [matters of] pride or arrogance", Rādhā (RS2). **मदालस** (*madālasa*) M.

मधुरिपु (*madhuripu*) M. "enemy of the demon Madhu", Viṣṇu (AK), Kṛṣṇa (ViP).

मनस्य (*manasya*) M. "he who thinks or reflects on", a *deva* (BrP). **मनस्या** (*manasyā*) F.

मनस्यु (*manasyu*) MF. "one who wishes or desires [something good]", a king (MBh).

मनस्विक (*manasvika*) M. "wise, clever, attentive, resolute", a *nāga* (VāP). **मनस्विका** (*manasvikā*) F.

मनुग (*manuga*) M. "he who follows his thinking or the wise", a king (VāP). **मनुगा** (*manugā*) F.

मनुविद्या (*manuvidyā*) F. "one of the twelve types of *śrīvidyā*", Lalitā (LS1).

मनोजव (*manojava*) M. "with the speed of the mind, quick, swift", Viṣṇu (VS1), Śiva (ŚS1). **मनोजवा** (*manojavā*) F. Lakṣmī (LS2).

मनोनुग (*manonuga*) M. "he who follows his mind", a king (BrP). **मनोनुगा** (*manonugā*) F.

मनोभवा (*manobhavā*) F. "existing in the mind", Lakṣmī (LS2). **मनोभव** (*manobhava*) M.

मनोमयी (*manomayī*) F. "spiritual, mental", Yamunā (YS), Lalitā (LS1). **मनोमय** (*manomaya*) M. Gaṇeśa (GS6).

मनोवती (*manovatī*) F. "high-minded, wise", daughter of Tumburu (VāP). **मनोवान्** (*manovān*) M.

मनोवेग (*manovega*) M. "having the speed of the mind", Śiva (ŚS1). **मनोवेगा** (*manovegā*) F.

मन्त्रय (*mantraya*) M. "he who deliberates or counsels", son of Kṛṣṇa (VāP). **मन्त्रया** (*mantrayā*) F.

मन्त्रवित्/मन्त्रविद् (*mantravit/mantravid*) MF. "the knower of *mantras*", Śiva (ŚS1), son of Kṛṣṇa (BrP), similar to the name *tantra-mantra-viśeṣajñā* of Gāyatrī (GS4).

मन्त्रिणी (*mantriṇī*) F. "she whose *mantra* is praiseworthy", Lakṣmī (LS3). **मन्त्री** (*mantrī*) M.

मन्थु (*manthu*) MF. "one who thinks, a thinker", a king (BhP).

मन्दगा (*mandagā*) F. "she who moves slowly (=gracefully)", a river (BrP). **मन्दग** (*mandaga*) M.

मन्दस्मित (*mandasmita*) M. "gently smiling", Kṛṣṇa (KS2). **मन्दस्मिता** (*mandasmitā*) F.

मन्युमान् (*manyumān*) M. "ardent, passionate, energetic", an *agni* (MBh). **मन्युमती** (*manyumatī*) F.

मयस्कर (*mayaskara*) M. "he who causes (=bestows) the bliss of *mokṣa*", used for Rudra (ŚYM). **मयस्करी** (*mayaskarī*) F.

मयोभव (*mayobhava*) M. "the origin or source of [worldly and divine] bliss", used for Rudra (ŚYM). **मयोभवा** (*mayobhavā*) F.

मयोभुव (*mayobhuva*) M. "gladdening, delighting", a *ṛṣi* (MaP). **मयोभुवा** (*mayobhuvā*) F.

मरीचिमान् (*marīcimān*) M. "having rays, brilliant, radiant", a *vānara* (BrP). **मरीचिमती** (*marīcimatī*) F.

मरुत्वान् (*marutvān*) M. "having the *Maruts*", Sūrya (SS1).

मरुत्वती (*marutvatī*) F.

मसृण (*masṛṇa*) M. "charming, sweet, beaming", a *ṛṣi* (MaP). **मसृणा** (*masṛṇā*) F.

महनीया (*mahanīyā*) F. "deserving praise or honour, illustrious", Lalitā (LS1). **महनीय** (*mahanīya*) M.

महस्वान् (*mahasvān*) M. "great, brilliant, lustrous", a king (BhP). **महस्वती** (*mahasvatī*) F.

महस्वी (*mahasvī*) M. "radiant, splendid, brilliant", Mṛtyuñjaya (MS1). **महस्विनी** (*mahasvinī*) F.

महाकेतु (*mahāketu*) MF. "with a great flag/banner", Śiva (ŚS1).

महाक्रम (*mahākrama*) M. "having great or large strides [as Vāmana]", Viṣṇu (VS1). **महाक्रमा** (*mahākramā*) F.

महाक्ष (*mahākṣa*) M. "great-eyed", Viṣṇu (VS1), Śiva (ŚS1). **महाक्षी** (*mahākṣī*) F.

महागम (*mahāgama*) M. "with great learning", Hanumān (HS). **महागमा** (*mahāgamā*) F.

महाङ्ग (*mahāṅga*) M. "with a great body or limbs", Śiva (ŚS1). **महाङ्गी** (*mahāṅgī*) F.

महाद्युति (*mahādyuti*) MF. "with great brilliance", Viṣṇu (VS1).

महाधन (*mahādhana*) M. "he from whom great *dhanas* (treasures or riches) [emanate]", Viṣṇu (VS1), Śiva (ŚS2). **महाधना** (*mahādhanā*) F. Lakṣmī (LS2).

महामनस् (*mahāmanas*) MF. "high-minded, magnanimous", a king (BhP).

महायशस् (*mahāyaśas*) MF. "of great renown, illustrious", Śiva (ŚS1).

महायुध (*mahāyudha*) M. "great warrior, with a great weapon", Śiva (ŚS1). **महायुधा** (*mahāyudhā*) F.

महारथ (*mahāratha*) M. "with a great chariot [in the form of the earth]", Śiva (ŚS1). **महारथा** (*mahārathā*) F.

महार्ह (*mahārha*) M. "extremely worthy or deserving", Viṣṇu (VS1). **महार्हा** (*mahārhā*) F.

महालय (*mahālaya*) M. "the great place of refuge", Sūrya (SS1). **महालया** (*mahālayā*) F.

महावेग (*mahāvega*) M. "having great speed or velocity", Śiva (ŚS1). **महावेगा** (*mahāvegā*) F. Durgā (DS3).

महाशन (*mahāśana*) M. "devouring a lot (consuming everything at the time of *pralaya*)", Viṣṇu (VS1), Sūrya (SS1). **महाशना** (*mahāśanā*) F.

महास्वन (*mahāsvana*) M. "having a great sound (=voice)", Viṣṇu (VS1). **महास्वना** (*mahāsvanā*) F.

महीयसी (*mahīyasī*) F. "greater, larger, more important", Sītā (SS2). **महीयान्** (*mahīyān*) M.

महेज्य (*mahejya*) M. "greatly honourable, he whose worship is great, highly worthy of worship", Viṣṇu (VS1). **महेज्या**

(*mahejyā*) F. Bhavānī (BS).

महोक्ष (*mahokṣa*) M. "very large, the great cleanser [of *pāpas*]", Hanumān (HS). **महोक्षा** (*mahokṣā*) F.

महोग्र (*mahogra*) M. "greatly formidable or fierce", Sūrya (SS1). **महोग्रा** (*mahogrā*) F.

महोज्ज्वल (*mahojjvala*) M. "greatly luminous or splendid", Narasiṃha (NS). **महोज्ज्वला** (*mahojjvalā*) F.

महोदर (*mahodara*) M. "with an excellent belly, great in a battle or war", Śiva (ŚS1), Rāma (RS1), Narasiṃha (NS). **महोदरी** (*mahodarī*) F.

महोन्नता (*mahonnatā*) F. "very high, lofty", Yamunā (YS). **महोन्नत** (*mahonnata*) M.

महोरस्क (*mahoraska*) M. "broad-chested", Śiva (ŚS1), Rāma (RS1). **महोरस्का** (*mahoraskā*) F.

महौजस् (*mahaujas*) MF. "with great *ojas*, very mighty", a *deva* (BrP).

मागधी (*māgadhī*) F. "a panegyrist, she who sings praises", Gāyatrī (GS4). **मागध** (*māgadha*) M.

माङ्गल्य (*māṅgalya*) M. "possessing auspiciousness", Sūrya (SS1). **माङ्गल्या** (*maṅgalyā*) F.

माण्डूकि (*māṇḍūki*) M. "the son of Māṇḍūka", a *ṛṣi* (BrP). **माण्डूकी** (*māṇḍūkī*) .

माध्वीक (*mādhvīka*) M. "possessing *madhu* (the nectar of flowers), sweet", Kṛṣṇa (KS2). **माध्वीका** (*mādhvīkā*) F.

मानदा (*mānadā*) F. "giving honour or respect", Yamunā (YS). **मानद** (*mānada*) M.

मानवती (*mānavatī*) F. "high-minded, honourable", Lalitā (LS1). **मानवान्** (*mānavān*) M.

मानित (*mānita*) M. "honoured, respected, esteemed", used for Balarāma (BhP). **मानिता** (*mānitā*) F.

मायातीत (*māyātīta*) M. "beyond *māyā*", Narasiṃha (NS). **मायातीता** (*māyātītā*) F.

मारुतेश/मारुतेश्वर (*māruteśa/māruteśvara*) M. "the lord of all *mārutas* (*maruts*)", Vāyu (BrP). **मारुतेश्वरी** (*māruteśvarī*) F.

माहेयी (*māheyī*) F. "daughter of the earth", Rādhā (RS2), Gomātā (AK). **माहेय** (*māheya*) M.

मित्रवान् (*mitravān*) M. "having many/praiseworthy friends", a *deva* (MBh). **मित्रवती** (*mitravatī*) F.

मित्राभ (*mitrābha*) M. "he whose lustre is like that of Sūrya". **मित्राभा** (*mitrābhā*) F.

मित्रायु (*mitrāyu*) MF. "seeking friends", a king (BhP).

मित्रेयु (*mitreyu*) MF. "desiring friends", a clan of Bhārgavas (BrP).

मिहिराण (*mihirāṇa*) M. "he who is praised or eulogized by *mihira* (Sūrya)", Śiva (TK). **मिहिराणा** (*mihirāṇā*) F.

मीनेशी (*mīneśī*) F. "the goddess of fishes", Rādhā (RS2). **मीनेश** (*mīneśa*) M.

मुख्या (*mukhyā*) F. "principal, primary", Yamunā (YS). **मुख्य** (*mukhya*) M.

मुचिर (*mucira*) M. "liberal, munificent" (TK). **मुचिरा** (*mucirā*) F.

मुञ्जकेश (*muñjakeśa*) M. "he whose hair is [sacred] like the *muñja* grass", Viṣṇu (VS2), Śiva (ŚS4). **मुञ्जकेशी** (*muñjakeśī*) F.

मुदाकरी (*mudākarī*) F. "causing happiness", Gaṅgā (GS3). **मुदाकर** (*mudākara*) M.

मुद्रास्या (*mudrāsyā*) F. "with a delightful face", Rādhā (RS2). **मुद्रास्य** (*mudrāsya*) M.

मूर्धन्या (*mūrdhanyā*) F. "being at the head (=in the front), eminent, excellent", used in HD. **मूर्धन्य** (*mūrdhanya*) M.

मृडानी (*mṛḍānī*) F. "wife of Mṛḍa=Śiva", Bhavānī (BS), Lalitā (LS1). **मृड** (*mṛḍa*) M. Śiva (ŚS2, ŚS3).

मेधज (*medhaja*) M. "manifesting in *yajñas*", Viṣṇu (VS1). **मेधजा** (*medhajā*) F.

मेधाद (*medhāda*) M. "the bestower of intellect", Hanumān (HS). **मेधादा** (*medhādā*) F.

मेधावान् (*medhāvān*) M. "he whose *medhā* (intelligence or retentive power) is praiseworthy, intelligent, wise", a *deva* (VāP). **मेधावती** (*medhāvatī*) F.

मेधिक (*medhika*) M. "possessing an offering or yajña", Sūrya (SS1). **मेधिका** (*medhikā*) F.

मेधिर (*medhira*) M. "possessing *medhā* (intellect or retentive power), wise, intelligent", used for Agni (ṚVŚ). **मेधिरा** (*medhirā*) F.

मेध्य (*medhya*) M. "pure, strong, wise", Sūrya (SS1). **मेध्या** (*medhyā*) F. Gaṅgā (GS3).

मेरुजा (*merujā*) F. "daughter of Meru", similar to name *merutanayā* of Gāyatrī (GS4). **मेरुज** (*meruja*) M.

मोक्षद (*mokṣada*) M. "granting *mokṣa*", Rāma (RS1). **मोक्षदा** (*mokṣadā*) F.

मोचिका (*mocikā*) F. "she who liberates or emancipates", a *śakti* (BrP). **मोचक** (*mocaka*) M.

मोदिता (*moditā*) F. "delighted, joyous, fragrant". **मोदित** (*modita*) M.

मोदिनी (*modinī*) F. "blissful, gladdening, delighting", Annapūrṇā (AS). **मोदी** (*modī*) M.

यक्षेश/यक्षेश्वर (*yakṣeśa/yakṣeśvara*) M. "lord of *yakṣas*", *yakṣeśvara* is Kubera (BrP). **यक्षेशी/यक्षेश्वरी** (*yakṣeśī/yakṣeśvarī*) F. Bhadrā is the wife of Kubera (MBh).

यजनी (*yajanī*) F. "she who performs *yajñas*", wife of Śukra (VāP). **यजन** (*yajana*) M.

यजुदाय (*yajudāya*) M. "he who gifts or presents *yajus* (mantras of Yajurveda)", son of Devakī (VāP).

यजुर्मय (*yajurmaya*) M. "consisting of mantras of Yajurveda, he whose form (*svarūpa*) is the Yajurveda", Śiva (ŚS4). **यजुर्मयी** (*yajurmayī*) F.

यज्ञेशी (*yajñeśī*) F. "the goddess of *yajñas*", Gaṅgā (GS3). **यज्ञेश** (*yajñeśa*) M.

यज्वा (*yajvā*) M. "[having the form of] the performer of *yajñas*", Viṣṇu (VS1), Rāma (RS1). **यज्वरी** (*yajvarī*) F.

यदुवर (*yaduvara*) M. "the best among the Yadus", Kṛṣṇa (MBh).

यन्त्रिणी (*yantriṇī*) F. "she who possesses the *yantra*", attendant of Lalitā (BrP). **यन्त्री** (*yantrī*) M.

यविष्ठ (*yaviṣṭha*) M. "the youngest, very young", a *deva* (VāP). **यविष्ठा** (*yaviṣṭhā*) F.

यवीयान् (*yavīyān*) M. "younger, very young", a *deva* (BrP). **यवीयसी** (*yavīyasī*) F.

यशस्करी (*yaśaskarī*) F. "the cause of fame or renown", Gaṅgā (GS3), Lakṣmī (LS2). **यशस्कर** (*yaśaskara*) M. Hanumān (HS), Gaṇeśa (GS2).

यशस्विज (*yaśasvija*) M. "distinguished by fame or renown", a *deva* (BrP). **यशस्विजा** (*yaśasvijā*) F.

यशोवती (*yaśovatī*) F. "famous, renowned", Lakṣmī (LS2). **यशोवान्** (*yaśovān*) M.

याच्या (*yācyā*) F. "worth asking from", Gaṅgā (GS3). **याच्य** (*yācya*) M.

याजक (*yājaka*) M. "he who worships", Hanumān (HS). **याजिका** (*yājikā*) F.

याजुषी (*yājuṣī*) F. "associated with Yajurveda", Gāyatrī (GS4). **याजुष** (*yājuṣa*) M.

युगावर्त (*yugāvarta*) M. "setting the *yugas* in motion", Viṣṇu (VS1), Śiva (ŚS3), Sūrya (SS1). **युगावर्ता** (*yugāvartā*) F.

युगावह (*yugāvaha*) M. "bringing about the *yugas*", Śiva (ŚS1). **युगावहा** (*yugāvahā*) F.

युधामन्यु (*yudhāmanyu*) MF. "furious or raging in battle", a warrior (MBh).

युयुत्सु (*yuyutsu*) MF. "desirous to fight, a warrior", son of Dhṛtarāṣṭra who joined the Pāṇḍavas (MBh).

युयुध (*yuyudha*) M. "eager to fight, a warrior", a king (BhP). **युयुधा** (*yuyudhā*) F.

युयुधान (*yuyudhāna*) M. "he who fights, a warrior", name of Sātyaki (MBh). **युयुधाना** (*yuyudhānā*) F.

योक्त्री (*yoktrī*) F. "she who joins or unites", Lakṣmī (LS2). **योक्ता** (*yoktā*) M.

योगजा (*yogajā*) F. "born from or with *yoga*, a born *yoginī*", Pārvatī (PS). **योगज** (*yogaja*) M.

योगदा (*yogadā*) F. "she who bestows *yoga* (the state of union)",

Lalitā (LS1), Sītā (SS2), Sarasvatī (SS3), Yamunā (YS). **योगद** (*yogada*) M.

योगमय (*yogamaya*) M. "consisting of *yoga*, full of *yoga*", Viṣṇu (VS2). **योगमयी** (*yogamayī*) F.

योगस्था (*yogasthā*) F. "situated in *yoga*", Sītā (SS2). **योगस्थ** (*yogastha*) M. In the BG, Kṛṣṇa instructs Arjuna to perform actions while being *yogastha.*

योगाङ्गा (*yogāṅgā*) F. "she whose limbs (body) are (is) endowed with *yoga*", Bhavānī (BS). **योगाङ्ग** (*yogāṅga*) M.

योगेशी (*yogeśī*) F. "goddess of *yoga*", Rādhā (RS2). **योगेश** (*yogeśa*) M.

योज्य (*yojya*) M. "worth uniting/connecting [with]", Śiva (ŚS1). **योज्या** (*yojyā*) F.

योधिका (*yodhikā*) F. "she who fights, a female warrior", listed in KRM. **योधक** (*yodhaka*) M. used for warriors in MBh.

यौधेय (*yaudheya*) M. "he who deserves to fight, a warrior", son of Yudhiṣṭhira (MBh). **यौधेयी** (*yaudheyī*) F.

रक्षोघ्न (*rakṣoghna*) M. "destroyer of *rākṣasas* (demons)", Sūrya (SS1), Rāma (RS1), Narasiṃha (NS), Hanumān (HS). **रक्षोघ्नी** (*rakṣoghnī*) F. Bhavānī (BS).

रङ्गिणी (*raṅgiṇī*) F. "with attachment or love, passionate", Yamunā (YS). **रङ्गी** (*raṅgī*) M.

रजेयु (*rajeyu*) MF. "desirous of *rajas* (the quality of passion)", a king (VāP).

रञ्जक (*rañjaka*) M. "he who colours or pleases", Kṛṣṇa (KS2), Gaṇeśa (GS2). **रञ्जिका** (*rañjikā*) F.

रणेजय (*raṇejaya*) M. "victorious in battles", a king (MaP). **रणेजया** (*raṇejayā*) F.

रण्विता (*raṇvitā*) F. "invoked, praised, or eulogized", used for Uṣas and Nakta (the dawn and night deities) in ṚVŚ. **रण्वित** (*raṇvita*) M.

रत्नदा (*ratnadā*) F. "bestower of jewels", Lakṣmī (LS2). **रत्नद** (*ratnada*) M.

रत्नाङ्ग (*ratnāṅga*) M. "he whose limbs are ornamented or [brilliant] like ornaments", Śiva (ŚS1). **रत्नाङ्गी** (*ratnāṅgī*) F.

रथस्था (*rathasthā*) F. "seated on a chariot", Yamunā (YS). **रथस्थ** (*rathastha*) M.

रन्तिदेव (*rantideva*) M. "the god of pleasure or sport", a king (MBh, BhP). **रन्तिदेवी** (*rantidevī*) F.

रम्यक (*ramyaka*) M. "delightful, agreeable, pleasing, lovely", a king (BhP). **रम्यका** (*ramyakā*) F.

रविज (*ravija*) M. "son of Sūrya", Kṛṣṇa (KS2). **रविजा** (*ravijā*) F.

रागेशी (*rāgeśī*) F. "goddess of affection or *rāgas*", Gāyatrī (GS4). **रागेश** (*rāgeśa*) M.

राज्यदा (*rājyadā*) F. "bestower of kingdoms", Gāyatrī (GS4).

राज्यद (*rājyada*) M.

रामेष्ट (*rāmeṣṭa*) M. "he whose *iṣṭa* is Rāma", Hanumān (HS). **रामेष्टा** (*rāmeṣṭā*) F.

रिवेयु (*riveyu*) MF. "desirous of going (=knowing)", a *rājarṣi* (VāP).

रुक्मेषु (*rukmeṣu*) MF. "having arrows of gold", a king (BhP).

रुचक (*rucaka*) M. "agreeable, pleasing", a king (BhP). **रुचिका** (*rucikā*) F.

रुद्राम्बा (*rudrāmbā*) F. "mother of the Rudras", the mother of Rudras is *go* (the cow or divine speech) as per ṚVŚ.

रुद्रेशी (*rudreśī*) F. "goddess of *rudras*", *mātṛkā* or mother goddess (MaP). **रुद्रेश** (*rudreśa*) M.

रुशङ्कु (*ruśaṅku*) MF. "like a spear in the battle (=swift and piercing)", a king (ViP).

रुशद्रथ (*ruśadratha*) M. "with a bright chariot", a king (BhP). **रुशद्रथा** (*ruśadrathā*) F.

रेचिका (*recikā*) F. "she who clears, empties, or purges [*pāpas*]", a *śakti* (BrP). **रेचक** (*recaka*) M.

रेवतीश (*revatīśa*) M. "the lord (=husband) of Revatī", Balarāma (AgP).

रैवत (*raivata*) M. "wealthy, splendid, beautiful", Śiva (TK), one of the Rudras (BhP). **रैवती** (*raivatī*) F.

रोचमान (*rocamāna*) M. "shining, brilliant, charming", a *viśvedeva* (BrP, MaP, VāP). **रोचमाना** (*rocamānā*) F.

रोचिका (*rocikā*) F. "shining, resplendent, brilliant", one of the ten worlds of the Śiva-tattva as per Tantra works. **रोचक** (*rocaka*) M.

रोचिष (*rociṣa*) M. "brilliant, splendid", son of Vibhāvasu (BhP). **रोचिषा** (*rociṣā*) F.

रोचिष्णु (*rociṣṇu*) MF. "shining, brilliant, splendid", Sūrya (SS1), Rāma (RS1), Hanumān (HS).

रोचिष्मती (*rociṣmatī*) F. "having light or splendour, brilliant", Lakṣmī (LS2). **रोचिष्मान्** (*rociṣmān*) M. son of second Manu (BhP).

रौच्य (*raucya*) M. "son of Ruci, coming from light", the ninth Manu (BrP). **रौची** (*raucī*) F.

रौद्र (*raudra*) M. "fierce, terrifying", a *vānara* (BrP). **रौद्री** (*raudrī*) F. a *śakti* (BrP).

रौहिणेय (*rauhiṇeya*) M. "son of Rohiṇī", Viṣṇu (VS2), Kṛṣṇa (KS2), Balarāma (MBh). **रौहिणेयी** (*rauhiṇeyī*) F.

लङ्कारि (*laṅkāri*) M. "the enemy of Laṅkā", Hanumān (HS).

लभ्या (*labhyā*) F. "worth acquiring or obtaining, suitable", Durgā (DS3). **लभ्य** (*labhya*) M.

लम्बन (*lambana*) M. "he from whom hang (emanate) many *brahmāṇḍas*", Śiva (ŚS1). **लम्बनी** (*lambanī*) F.

लवित्र (*lavitra*) M. "he who cuts or tears off", Narasiṃha (NS).

लसिता (*lasitā*) F. "shining, playing, sportive", part of the name *svarṇa-lasitā* of Durgā (DS4). **लसित** (*lasita*) M.

लाक्षकी (*lākṣakī*) F. "having lakhs [of attendants]", Sītā (ŚK). **लाक्षक** (*lākṣaka*) M.

लास्यप्रिया (*lāsyapriyā*) F. "she who likes *lāsya* (the divine dance)", Lalitā (LS1). **लास्यप्रिय** (*lāsyapriya*) M.

लीलाक्ष (*līlākṣa*) M. "with playful or sportive eyes", Kṛṣṇa (KS1). **लीलाक्षी** (*līlākṣī*) F.

लेखिनी (*lekhinī*) F. "she who writes or paints", a *devī* (MaP). **लेखी** (*lekhī*) M.

लोकिनी (*lokinī*) F. "possessing [all the] worlds or realms", Gāyatrī (GS4). **लोकी** (*lokī*) M.

लोकेशी (*lokeśī*) F. "ruler of the worlds", part of the name *sarva-lokeśī* of Lalitā (LS1). **लोकेश** (*lokeśa*) M.

लोलाक्षी (*lolākṣī*) F. "with rolling (playful) eyes", Bhavānī (BS), part of name *lolākṣī-kāmarūpiṇī* of Lalitā (LS1). **लोलाक्ष** (*lolākṣa*) M. Mṛtyuñjaya (MS1).

लोहिताक्ष (*lohitākṣa*) M. "with red eyes", Viṣṇu (VS1). **लोहिताक्षी** (*lohitākṣī*) F.

लौहित्य (*lauhitya*) M. "having redness, reddish in complexion", a *śrutarṣi* (BrP). **लौहित्या** (*lauhityā*) F.

वज्राङ्ग (*vajrāṅga*) M. "he whose limbs (body) are (is) [strong] like the *vajra*", Hanumān (HS). **वज्राङ्गी** (*vajrāṅgī*) F.

वज्रायुध (*vajrāyudha*) M. "he whose weapon is the *vajra*", used for Indra (BhP). **वज्रायुधा** (*vajrāyudhā*) F. Bhavānī (BS).

वज्रिणी (*vajriṇī*) F. "bearing the *vajra*", Gāyatrī (GS4). **वज्री** (*vajrī*) M. Indra (AK), Śiva (ŚS1, ŚS5).

वज्रेशी (*vajreśī*) F. "goddess of *vajra*", Lalitā (BrP), similar to name *vajreśvarī* of Lalitā (LS1). **वज्रेश** (*vajreśa*) M.

वत्सर (*vatsara*) M. "the location of everything", Viṣṇu (VS1), Narasiṃha (NS).

वदान्य (*vadānya*) M. "eloquent, liberal, munificent", Sūrya (SS1), a *ṛṣi* whose daughter Aṣṭāvakra married (MBh). **वदान्या** (*vadānyā*) F. Bhavānī (BS).

वनेयु (*vaneyu*) MF. "wishing for the forest", a king (BhP).

वपुष्मती (*vapuṣmatī*) F. "she whose form/body is praiseworthy (=beautiful/handsome)", a river (VāP). **वपुष्मान्** (*vapuṣmān*) M. a king (BrP).

वराङ्ग (*varāṅga*) M. "with an excellent body or form", Viṣṇu (VS1). **वराङ्गी** (*varāṅgī*) F. a queen (BrP).

वराङ्गना (*varāṅganā*) F. "the best lady, a lovely lady", a princess (VāP).

वराङ्गा (*varāṅgā*) F. "having beautiful limbs or body", Yamunā (YS). **वराङ्ग** (*varāṅga*) M.

वरात्मा (*varātmā*) M. "the best *ātman*", Narasiṃha (NS).

वरानना (*varānanā*) F. "having a lovely face", an Apsaras (ViP). **वरानन** (*varānana*) M.

वरार्चिता (*varārcitā*) F. "worshipped by the best", Lakṣmī (LS2). **वरार्चित** (*varārcita*) M.

वरिष्ठा (*variṣṭhā*) F. "largest, most excellent, best", Gaṅgā (GS3), Lakṣmī (LS2). **वरिष्ठ** (*variṣṭha*) M. Narasiṃha (NS).

वरीयान् (*varīyān*) M. "larger, greater, very good", Śiva (ŚS3). **वरीयसी** (*varīyasī*) F.

वर्चला (*varcalā*) F. "possessing brilliance", Durgā (DS3). **वर्चल** (*varcala*) M.

वर्चस्करी (*varcaskarī*) F. "causing energy and light", Gaṅgā (GS3). **वर्चस्कर** (*varcaskara*) M.

वर्चस्वी (*varcasvī*) M. "possessing brightness or energy", Sūrya (SS1). **वर्चस्विनी** (*varcasvinī*) F.

वर्ण्य (*varṇya*) M. "worthy of being described", Rāma (RS1). **वर्ण्या** (*varṇyā*) F.

वर्तिनी (*vartinī*) F. "thriving, being [well]", Bhavānī (BS). **वर्ती** (*vartī*) M.

वर्धनीय (*vardhanīya*) M. "worthy of being pleased", Kṛṣṇa (KS2). **वर्धनीया** (*vardhanīyā*) F.

वर्धन्य (*vardhanya*) M. "skilled in growing or pleasing", Kṛṣṇa (KS2). **वर्धन्या** (*vardhanyā*) F.

वर्धित (*vardhita*) M. "gladdened", Kṛṣṇa (KS2). **वर्धिता**

(*vardhitā*) F.

वर्धिष्णु (*vardhiṣṇu*) MF. "one whose nature is to grow, increase, or expand", Viṣṇu (VS3), used in the *mudrā* (seal) of Chhatrapati Shivaji Maharaj to describe the *mudrā* itself.

वशक (*vaśaka*) M. "he who shines or wishes", Kṛṣṇa (KS1). **वशिका** (*vaśikā*) F.

वशङ्करी (*vaśaṅkarī*) F. "subduing, taking [others] under control", Sītā (SS2). **वशङ्कर** (*vaśaṅkara*) M.

वशिनी (*vaśinī*) F. "powerful, self-controlled", Sītā (SS2). **वशी** (*vaśī*) M.

वसुप्रद (*vasuprada*) M. "he who bestows riches or prosperity", Sūrya (SS1). **वसुप्रदा** (*vasupradā*) F. Lakṣmī (LS2).

वसुमान् (*vasumān*) M. "possessing wealth", Sūrya (SS1), Viṣṇu (VS1). **वसुमती** (*vasumatī*) F.

वसुमित्र (*vasumitra*) M. "a friend of *vasu* (wealth or Agni), prosperous or performing *yajñas*", a king (BhP). **वसुमित्रा** (*vasumitrā*) F.

वसुमोद (*vasumoda*) M. "he who gets pleasure from *vasu* or Agni (=performing *yajñas*)", a king (VāP). **वसुमोदा** (*vasumodā*) F.

वाक्पति (*vākpati*) M. "the master of speech", Bṛhaspati (MaP, VāP).

वागुरा (*vāgurā*) F. "she who binds [the evil]", Bhavānī (BS). **वागुर** (*vāgura*) M.

वाग्ग्मी (*vāggmī*) M. "speaking well, eloquent", Kṛṣṇa (KS1), Hanumān (HS), used for Rāma (VR). **वाग्ग्मिनी** (*vāggminī*) F.

वाङ्मय (*vāṅmaya*) M. "made of or endowed with [divine] speech, eloquent", Rāma (RS1). **वाङ्मयी** (*vāṅmayī*) F. Sarasvatī (SS3).

वाच्या (*vācyā*) F. "worth being spoken about", Sītā (SS2). **वाच्य** (*vācya*) M.

वाजसन (*vājasana*) M. "bestower of grain, belonging to *Vājasaneyas*", Viṣṇu (VS1), Śiva (ŚS1).

वात्यावी (*vātyāvī*) F. "she from whom the strong winds flow", Bhavānī (BS).

वादिनी (*vādinī*) F. "eloquent, she who speaks pleasantly", Lakṣmī (LS3). **वादी** (*vādī*) M.

वामदेवी (*vāmadevī*) F. "the beautiful goddess", Gaṅgā (GS3), Lalitā (LS1), Rādhā (RS2). **वामदेव** (*vāmadeva*) M. Śiva (ŚS1).

वामेशी (*vāmeśī*) F. "the beautiful goddess", Lakṣmī (LS2). **वामेश** (*vāmeśa*) M.

वायवी (*vāyavī*) F. "related to Vāyu, pervading the wind element", Yamunā (YS). **वायव/वायव्य** (*vāyava/vāyavya*) M.

वायुगा (*vāyugā*) F. "she who goes with the wind, travelling through air", Lakṣmī (LS3). **वायुग** (*vāyuga*) M.

वारिमेजय (*vārimejaya*) M. "he who makes the waters tremble", a prince (MaP). **वारिमेजया** (*vārimejayā*) F.

वारुणीश (*vāruṇīśa*) M. "the lord of *vāruṇī* (a drink personified as the wife of Balarāma)", Viṣṇu (VS2). **वारुणीशी** (*vāruṇīśī*) F.

विकर्तन (*vikartana*) M. "he who cuts, divides, or tears apart [darkness or clouds]", Sūrya (AK), Mṛtyuñjaya (MS1). **विकर्तनी** (*vikartanī*) F.

विकर्म/विकर्मा (*vikarma/vikarmā*) M. "with special actions", Narasiṃha (NS). **विकर्मा** (*vikarmā*) F.

विक्षर (*vikṣara*) M. "free from destruction", Viṣṇu (VS1). **विक्षरा** (*vikṣarā*) F.

विग्रहा (*vigrahā*) F. "having a [praiseworthy] form, specially receiving [prayers]", Bhavānī (BS). **विग्रह** (*vigraha*) M.

विचक्षण (*vicakṣaṇa*) M. "far-sighted, wise, clever, skilful", Sūrya (SS1), Śiva (ŚS3). **विचक्षणा** (*vicakṣaṇā*) F.

विचित्राङ्गी (*vicitrāṅgī*) F. "with beautiful limbs or body", Gaṅgā (GS3), Sītā (SS2). **विचित्राङ्ग** (*vicitrāṅga*) M.

विजिगीषु (*vijigīṣu*) MF. "desirous of victory, warrior", used for the victorious king (MaP).

विज्ञात्री (*vijñātrī*) F. "she who knows or perceives, with special knowledge", Lalitā (LS1). **विज्ञाता** (*vijñātā*) M.

विज्वर (*vijvara*) M. "free from illnesses or anxieties", Dattātreya (DS2). **विज्वरा** (*vijvarā*) F.

वितृष्णा (*vitṛṣṇā*) F. "satisfied, content, without desires", a river (VāP). **वितृष्ण** (*vitṛṣṇa*) M.

वित्तवान् (*vittavān*) M. "possessing wealth, prosperous, rich", son of Raivata Manu (MaP). **वित्तवती** (*vittavatī*) F.

विदग्ध (*vidagdha*) M. "clever, shrewd", Narasiṃha (NS). **विदग्धा** (*vidagdhā*) F. Lalitā (LS1).

विदथ (*vidatha*) M. "wise, learned, scholar", used many times in ṚVŚ, a *yogī* (MK).

विदथ्य (*vidathya*) M. "skilled in knowledge, assembly, *yajña*, or battle", used variously in ṚVŚ, ŚYM, AVŚ. **विदथ्या** (*vidathyā*) F. used in ṚVŚ.

विदुत्तमा (*viduttamā*) F. "the best among the learned ones", Rādhā (RS2). **विदुत्तम** (*viduttama*) M.

विदूरथ (*vidūratha*) M. "he whose warriors are intelligent", a king (BhP). **विदूरथा** (*vidūrathā*) F.

विदेहजा (*videhajā*) F. "daughter of Videha (=Janaka)", Sītā (BrP).

विद्यामय (*vidyāmaya*) M. "consisting of (=rich in) knowledge", Mṛtyuñjaya (MS1). **विद्यामयी** (*vidyāmayī*) F. Durgā (DS4), Sītā (SS2).

विद्याराज (*vidyārāja*) M. "the king (=master) of knowledge", Viṣṇu (VS2).

विद्यावी (*vidyāvī*) F. "she from whom learning flows", Annapūrṇā (AS).

विद्योत (*vidyota*) M. "flashing, brillant", son of Dharma or

Yama (BhP). **विद्योता** (*vidyotā*) F.

विद्योतन (*vidyotana*) M. "especially brilliant or illuminating", Sūrya (SS1). **विद्योतनी** (*vidyotanī*) F.

विधूदय (*vidhūdaya*) M. "having the *udaya* (brilliance) of the moon", Kṛṣṇa (KS2).

विधेय (*vidheya*) M. "obedient", Sūrya (SS1), Narasiṃha (NS). **विधेया** (*vidheyā*) F.

विनिद्रा (*vinidrā*) F. "free from sleep (=ignorance), awake (=enlightened)", Bhavānī (BS). **विनिद्र** (*vinidra*) M.

विपक्व (*vipakva*) M. "especially developed, mature", a *deva* (BrP). **विपक्वा** (*vipakvā*) F.

विपञ्ची (*vipañcī*) F. "she who spreads or expands [bliss or benevolence]", Bhavānī (BS), Gaṅgā (GS3). **विपञ्च** (*vipañca*) M.

विपश्चित् (*vipaścit*) MF. "learned, wise", Hanumān (HS).

विपाप्मा (*vipāpmā*) MF. "free from *pāpas* (evil or vices)", a king (MaP).

विपृथु (*vipṛthu*) MF. "especially large, great, or clever", a prince (MBh).

विभक्त (*vibhakta*) M. "different, multifarious, ornamented", Sūrya (SS1). **विभक्ता** (*vibhaktā*) F.

विभाग (*vibhāga*) M. "he who is divided [as *vyaṣṭi*], he whose divisions [of *guṇas* and *karmas*] are special", Śiva (ŚS1).

विभागा (*vibhāgā*) F.

विभावसु (*vibhāvasu*) MF. "having the wealth of light, brilliant, radiant", Sūrya (SS1).

विभ्रमा (*vibhramā*) F. "free from confusion or ignorance", Bhavānī (BS). **विभ्रम** (*vibhrama*) M.

विभ्राज (*vibhrāja*) M. "especially radiant", a king (MaP). **विभ्राजा** (*vibhrājā*) F.

विमत्सर (*vimatsara*) M. "free from envy", Hanumān (HS). **विमत्सरा** (*vimatsarā*) F.

विमन्यु (*vimanyu*) MF. "without anger of grief", Sūrya (SS1).

विमुक्त (*vimukta*) M. "especially liberated, he due to whom beings are especially liberated [by the experience of oneness with him]", Śiva (ŚS1, ŚS5). **विमुक्ता** (*vimuktā*) F.

विमोचन (*vimocana*) M. "especially liberating", Śiva (ŚS1). **विमोचनी** (*vimocanī*) F.

विमोहा (*vimohā*) F. "free from *moha* (confusion or bewilderment)", Rādhā (RS2). **विमोह** (*vimoha*) M.

विमोहिनी (*vimohinī*) F. "she who especially bewilders [the ignorant]", Annapūrṇā (AS). **विमोही** (*vimohī*) M.

वियोगी (*viyogī*) M. "separated [from the material world]", Mṛtyuñjaya (MS1). **वियोगिनी** (*viyoginī*) F.

विरक्त (*virakta*) M. "free from [mundane] passion or attachment, dispassionate, indifferent", Narasiṃha (NS).

विरक्ता (*viraktā*) F. Durgā (DS3), Sītā (SS2).

विरक्ष (*virakṣa*) M. "especially protecting", a king (VāP). **विरक्षा** (*virakṣā*) F.

विरजस्क (*virajaska*) M. "free from dust, passion, or the quality of *rajas*", son of Sāvarṇi Manu (BhP). **विरजस्का** (*virajaskā*) F.

विराव (*virāva*) M. "he whose sound is special", a *deva* (BrP). **विरावा** (*virāvā*) F.

विरोचन (*virocana*) M. "especially brilliant", Viṣṇu (VS1). **विरोचनी** (*virocanī*) F.

विलक्षण (*vilakṣaṇa*) M. "extraordinary, different, unusual, with special signs", Rāma (RS1). **विलक्षणा** (*vilakṣaṇā*) F.

विलोचन (*vilocana*) M. "having a special vision", Sūrya (SS1). **विलोचना** (*vilocanā*) F.

विवक्षु (*vivakṣu*) MF. "desirous of speaking, eloquent", a king (MaP).

विवर्धन (*vivardhana*) M. "especially growing or increasing", Sūrya (SS1). **विवर्धनी** (*vivardhanī*) F.

विवस्वान् (*vivasvān*) M. "possessing light or brilliance", Sūrya (SS1), Rāma (RS1). **विवस्वती** (*vivasvatī*) F.

विविक्त (*vivikta*) M. "judicious, discriminative, solitary, pure, faultless", Viṣṇu (VS1), Rāma (RS1), Śiva (ŚS3). **विविक्ता** (*viviktā*) F.

विशारदा (*viśāradā*) F. "learned, wise, skilled, famous",

Bhavānī (BS). **विशारद** (*viśārada*) M.

विशालाक्ष (*viśālākṣa*) M. "with large eyes", Kṛṣṇa (KS2). **विशालाक्षी** (*viśālākṣī*) F.

विशिष्टा (*viśiṣṭā*) F. "superior, excellent", Sītā (SS2). **विशिष्ट** (*viśiṣṭa*) M.

विशोका (*viśokā*) F. "free from grief, blissful", Lakṣmī (LS2), Sītā (SS2), Rādhā (RS2). **विशोक** (*viśoka*) M.

विशोधन (*viśodhana*) M. "especially purifying", Viṣṇu (VS1). **विशोधनी** (*viśodhanī*) F. Gaṅgā (GS3).

विश्रवस् (*viśravas*) MF. "one of great fame or renown", a *ṛṣi* (BhP).

विश्वग (*viśvaga*) M. "he who goes everywhere (=omnipresent), he who knows everything (=omniscient)", a *ṛṣi* (BhP). **विश्वगा** (*viśvagā*) F.

विश्वप (*viśvapa*) M. "the protector of the world", Hanumān (HS). **विश्वपा** (*viśvapā*) F.

विश्वम्भरा (*viśvambharā*) F. "supporting or nourishing the world", the earth (AK), Lakṣmī (LS2). **विश्वम्भर** (*viśvambhara*) M.

विश्ववित्/विश्वविद् (*viśvavit/viśvavid*) MF. "knowing everything", Sūrya (SS1).

विश्वाची (*viśvācī*) F. "going everywhere, all-pervading", an Apsaras (BrP). **विश्वङ्** (*viśvaṅ*) M.

विश्वात्मा (*viśvātmā*) M. "the universal *ātman*", Viṣṇu (MBh).

विश्वायु (*viśvāyu*) MF. "seeking everything (or the world)", a king (VāP).

विश्वावसु (*viśvāvasu*) MF. "one whose wealth is everything, the source of everybody's wealth", Kṛṣṇa (MBh).

विश्वेशी (*viśveśī*) F. "goddess of the worlds", Gaṅgā (GS3). **विश्वेश** (*viśveśa*) M.

विषघ्नी (*viṣaghnī*) F. "she who destroys the poison [of ignorance or *saṃsāra*]", Gaṅgā (GS3), Sarasvatī (SS3). **विषघ्न** (*viṣaghna*) M.

विष्टुत (*viṣṭuta*) M. "especially praised", Sūrya (SS1). **विष्टुता** (*viṣṭutā*) F.

विष्णुरात (*viṣṇurāta*) M. "protected by Viṣṇu", Parīkṣit (BhP). **विष्णुराता** (*viṣṇurātā*) F.

विष्वक्सेन (*viṣvaksena*) M. "he whose army is everywhere", Viṣṇu (VS1), Śiva (ŚS1), Rāma (RS1), Kṛṣṇa (KS1), Narasiṃha (NS).

विसर्ग (*visarga*) M. "he whose creation is special", Śiva (ŚS1). **विसर्गा** (*visargā*) F.

विहग (*vihaga*) M. "moving in the sky", Sūrya (SS1). **विहगा** (*vihagā*) F.

विहायसी (*vihāyasī*) F. "heavenly, associated with (=situated in or moving in) *svarga* or sky", Yamunā (YS), Rādhā (RS2),

Sītā (SS2). **विहायस** (*vihāyasa*) M.

विहित (*vihita*) M. "appointed, placed", Sūrya (SS1). **विहिता** (*vihitā*) F.

विहितार्थ (*vihitārtha*) M. "he who apportions *arthas* (the four *puruṣārthas*)", Kṛṣṇa (KS1). **विहितार्था** (*vihitārthā*) F.

वीक्षा (*vīkṣā*) F. "she who has special sight, perception, or knowledge", Lakṣmī (LS2). **वीक्ष** (*vīkṣa*) M.

वीणावती (*vīṇāvatī*) F. "possessing (=playing) the *vīṇā*", Lalitā (BrP), Kālī (KS3). **वीणावान्** (*vīṇāvān*) M.

वीर्यवान् (*vīryavān*) M. "possessing strength, powerful, mighty", a *gandharva* (VāP). **वीर्यवती** (*vīryavatī*) F. one of the mother attendants of Skanda (MBh).

वृक्षायु (*vṛkṣāyu*) MF. "desiring trees, loving trees", son of Bāṣkala (VāP).

वृजिनी (*vṛjinī*) F. "liberal, sacrificing", daughter of Kṛṣṇa (BrP). **वृजी** (*vṛjī*) M.

वृता (*vṛtā*) F. "she who is chosen or selected", Yamunā (YS). **वृत** (*vṛta*) M.

वृद्धिदा (*vṛddhidā*) F. "the bestower of prosperity", Sarasvatī (SS3). **वृद्धिद** (*vṛddhida*) M.

वृन्देश (*vṛndeśa*) M. "lord of *vṛndā* (the sacred *tulasī*)", similar to name *vṛndāpati* of Kṛṣṇa (KS2). **वृन्देशी** (*vṛndeśī*) F.

वृष (*vṛṣa*) M. "he who showers (=fulfils wishes)", Viṣṇu

(VS1). **वृषा** (*vṛṣā*) F.

वेगवान् (*vegavān*) M. "swift, quick, possessing speed", Viṣṇu (VS1), Sūrya (SS1). **वेगवती** (*vegavatī*) F. Gaṅgā (GS3).

वेगिनी (*veginī*) F. "moving quickly, swift, quick", a *śakti* (BrP). **वेगी** (*vegī*) M.

वेणुमती (*veṇumatī*) F. "possessing a flute", a river (MaP). **वेणुमान्** (*veṇumān*) M. a king (BrP).

वेदगम्या (*vedagamyā*) F. "reachable through Vedas", Rādhā (RS2). **वेदगम्य** (*vedagamya*) M.

वेददर्श (*vedadarśa*) M. "he who sees (=knows) the Vedas", a *ṛṣi* (BhP).

वेदमय (*vedamaya*) M. "full of (=having the form of) Vedas", Mṛtyuñjaya (MS1), Narasiṃha (NS). **वेदमयी** (*vedamayī*) F. Sarasvatī (SS3), Gomātā (GS6).

वेदवित्/वेदविद् (*vedavit/vedavid*) MF. "one who knows the Vedas", Viṣṇu (VS1), Rāma (RS1), Śiva (ŚS2).

वेदवेद्य (*vedavedya*) M. "to be known by the Vedas", Kṛṣṇa (KS2). **वेदवेद्या** (*vedavedyā*) F.

वेदसार (*vedasāra*) M. "he whose essence is [expounded] in the Vedas", Viṣṇu (VS2). **वेदसारा** (*vedasārā*) F. Rādhā (RS2).

वेदस्तुत (*vedastuta*) M. "praised by the Vedas", Kṛṣṇa (RKS). **वेदस्तुता** (*vedastutā*) F.

वेदातीता (*vedātītā*) F. "beyond Vedas", Rādhā (RS2). **वेदातीत**

(*vedātīta*) M.

वेदाद्या (*vedādyā*) F. "the foremost in the Vedas", Rādhā (RKS). **वेदाद्य** (*vedādya*) M.

वेदार्था (*vedārthā*) F. "she whose meaning or signification is [expounded] in the Vedas", Durgā (DS3). **वेदार्थ** (*vedārtha*) M.

वेदिनी (*vedinī*) F. "she who knows, possessing the Vedas", Lakṣmī (LS3). **वेदी** (*vedī*) M.

वेद्य (*vedya*) M. "worth knowing", Viṣṇu (VS1), Sūrya (SS1), Rāma (RS1). **वेद्या** (*vedyā*) F. Gaṅgā (GS3).

वैखान (*vaikhāna*) M. "especially digging [as Varāha]", Viṣṇu (VS1).

वैदिकी (*vaidikī*) F. "associated with or knowing the Vedas", Yamunā (YS). **वैदिक** (*vaidika*) M.

वैद्युत (*vaidyuta*) M. "radiant, brilliant, resplendent", Narasiṃha (NS). **वैद्युती** (*vaidyutī*) F. Lakṣmī (LS2).

वैधृत (*vaidhṛta*) M. "possessing arrangement, orderly", Indra of the eleventh *manvantara* (BhP). **वैधृता** (*vaidhṛtā*) F. mother of Dharmasetu *avatāra* (BhP).

वैबुधी (*vaibudhī*) F. "divine, related to *devas*", Gaṅgā (GS3). **वैबुध** (*vaibudha*) M.

वैभासी (*vaibhāsī*) F. "daughter of *vibhāsa* = Sūrya", Yamunā (YS). **वैभास** (*vaibhāsa*) M.

वैयासकी (*vaiyāsakī*) F. "daughter of Vyāsa", Yamunā (YS).

वैयासकि (*vaiyāsaki*) M. Śukadeva (MBh, BhP).

वैरिमर्दन (*vairimardana*) M. "he who crushes his foes", Kṛṣṇa (KS2). **वैरिमर्दनी** (*vairimardanī*) F.

वैवस्वत (*vaivasvata*) M. "son of Vivasvān (Sūrya)", seventh Manu (BhP). **वैवस्वती** (*vaivasvatī*) F.

वैश्वानरी (*vaiśvānarī*) F. "belonging to all humans", Gaṅgā (GS3). **वैश्वानर** (*vaiśvānara*) M.

वैहायस (*vaihāyasa*) M. "dwelling or travelling in the sky", name of an aircraft (BhP). **वैहायसी** (*vaihāyasī*) F. a river (BhP).

व्यक्ता (*vyaktā*) F. "wise, learned, manifest", Lakṣmī (LS2). **व्यक्त** (*vyakta*) M.

व्यादिश (*vyādiśa*) M. "instructing, commanding [the *devas*]", Viṣṇu (VS1). **व्यादिशा** (*vyādiśā*) F.

व्यापक (*vyāpaka*) M. "pervading [everything]", Rāma (RS1), Kṛṣṇa (KS2), Hanumān (HS). **व्यापिका** (*vyāpikā*) F.

व्यापिनी (*vyāpinī*) F. "she who pervades [the worlds]", Gaṅgā (GS3), Lalitā (LS1), Lakṣmī (LS2), Sītā (SS2). **व्यापी** (*vyāpī*) M. Rāma (RS1), Kṛṣṇa (KS1).

व्याप्त (*vyāpta*) M. "pervading, omnipresent", Viṣṇu (VS1). **व्याप्ता** (*vyāptā*) F.

व्यालीन (*vyālīna*) M. "dense, united or combined [with Rādhā]", Kṛṣṇa (KS1). **व्यालीना** (*vyālīnā*) F.

व्युष्ट (*vyuṣṭa*) M. "bright, clear", son of Vibhāvasu (BhP). **व्युष्टा**

(*vyuṣṭā*) F.

व्युष्टि (*vyuṣṭi*) F. "she who has special beauty", Uṣas (ṚVŚ), a branch of *devas* (VāP).

व्यूहार्चित (*vyūhārcita*) M. "worshipped as the *vyūha*", Kṛṣṇa (KS2). **व्यूहार्चिता** (*vyūhārcitā*) F.

व्यूहेश (*vyūheśa*) M. "lord of *vyūhas* (the four manifestations, i.e. Balarāma, Pradyumna, Aniruddha, and Kṛṣṇa)", Kṛṣṇa (KS1). **व्यूहेशी** (*vyūheśī*) F.

व्येनी (*vyenī*) F. "especially white (=radiant or brilliant)", the dawn goddess Uṣas (ṚVŚ).

व्योमात्मा (*vyomātmā*) M. "the *ātman* of the sky", Narasiṃha (NS).

व्रतिनी (*vratinī*) F. "observing a [sacred or spiritual] vow, she whose vow is praiseworthy", Lakṣmī (LS3), queen of Kṛṣṇa (MaP). **व्रती** (*vratī*) M. Sūrya (SS1), a *yajamāna* (AK).

व्रतेयु (*vrateyu*) MF. "desirous of [observing] vows", a king (BhP).

शंवान् (*śaṃvān*) M. "possessing *śam*, auspicious, prosperous", example cited in Kāś. **शंवती** (*śaṃvatī*) F.

शक्तिदा (*śaktidā*) F. "the bestower of strength", Durgā (DS3). **शक्तिद** (*śaktida*) M.

शक्तिवर्धन (*śaktivardhana*) M. "increasing strength", a *ṛṣi* (MaP). **शक्तिवर्धनी** (*śaktivardhanī*) F.

शक्रानुज (*śakrānuja*) M. "the younger brother of Indra (as Vāmana)", Viṣṇu (MBh).

शतक्रतु (*śatakratu*) M. "he who has performed a hundred *yajñas*", Indra (MBh), Śiva (ŚS1).

शतघ्न (*śataghna*) M. "slaying one hundred [enemies at once]", a king (ViP). **शतघ्नी** (*śataghnī*) F.

शतजित् (*śatajit*) MF. "conquering one hundred [enemies]", son of Kṛṣṇa (BhP).

शततेजस् (*śatatejas*) MF. "having the might or brilliance of a hundred [people]", Vyāsa in the twelfth *Dvāpara* (VāP).

शतद्युम्न (*śatadyumna*) M. "having a hundred (= many) *dyumnas* (glories, powers, opulences, etc.)", a king (MBh). **शतद्युम्ना** (*śatadyumnā*) F.

शतानन्द (*śatānanda*) M. "he who gladdens hundreds (= many), he whose bliss is infinite", Viṣṇu (VS1), Gaṇeśa (GS2). **शतानन्दा** (*śatānandā*) F. Sītā (SS2), Yamunā (YS).

शतावर्ता (*śatāvartā*) F. "revolving hundreds [of entities]", Sītā (SS2). **शतावर्त** (*śatāvarta*) M. Viṣṇu (VS1), Śiva (ŚS4).

शत्रुजित् (*śatrujit*) MF. "conqueror of enemies", Viṣṇu (VS1), Rāma (RS1).

शर्याति (*śaryāti*) M. "one who moves with arrows", a king (MBh).

शर्वक (*śarvaka*) M. "he who goes [swiftly]", son of the Sahiṣṇu *avatāra* (VāP). **शर्विका** (*śarvikā*) F.

शर्वर (*śarvara*) M. "dark-complexioned", Kṛṣṇa (KS2). **शर्वरी** (*śarvarī*) F.

शान्तनुज (*śāntanuja*) M. "born from Śāntanu", Bhīṣma (MBh).

शान्तानुज (*śāntānuja*) M. "younger brother of Śāntā", Rāma (as per the VR).

शान्तिदा (*śāntidā*) F. "bestower of peace", Sītā (SS2). **शान्तिद** (*śāntida*) M.

शाम्बरी (*śāmbarī*) F. "magician, she who deludes [the ignorant]", Bhavānī (BS). **शाम्बर** (*śāmbara*) M.

शारदी (*śāradī*) F. "born in *śārad* season, new, modest", Yamunā (YS). **शारद** (*śārada*) M.

शालक (*śālaka*) M. "shining, brilliant", Gaṇeśa (GS2). **शालिका** (*śālikā*) F.

शाश्वती (*śāśvatī*) F. "everlasting, eternal", Lakṣmī (LS2), Annapūrṇā (AS). **शाश्वत** (*śāśvata*) M.

शिजय (*śijaya*) M. "he who wins with auspiciousness", a *rājarṣi* (VāP). **शिजया** (*śijayā*) F.

शितपु (*śitapu*) MF. "purifying the weak (=impure)", son of Uśanas (ViP).

शिवङ्करी (*śivaṅkarī*) F. "causing happiness or auspiciousness", Lalitā (LS1). **शिवङ्कर** (*śivaṅkara*) M.

शिवदा (*śivadā*) F. "she who bestows auspiciousness", Annapūrṇā (AS), Gaṅgā (GS3). **शिवद** (*śivada*) M.

शिवाख्या (*śivākhyā*) F. "having an auspicious name, having the name *Śivā*", Sītā (SS2), Pārvatī (PS). **शिवाख्य** (*śivākhya*) M.

शिवात्मक (*śivātmaka*) M. "having the nature of auspiciousness, Śiva himself", Kṛṣṇa (KS2). **शिवात्मिका** (*śivātmikā*) F.

शिवारम्भ (*śivārambha*) M. "he whose efforts are auspicious", Rāma (RS1). **शिवारम्भा** (*śivārambhā*) F.

शिवालय (*śivālaya*) M. "the abode, seat, place, or location of auspiciousness or Śivā (=Pārvatī)", Śiva (ŚS3). **शिवालया** (*śivālayā*) F. "the abode of auspiciousness" .

शिष्टेष्ट (*śiṣṭeṣṭa*) M. "worshipped by the learned and the virtuous, beloved of the noble ones", Viṣṇu (VS2). **शिष्टेष्टा** (*śiṣṭeṣṭā*) F. Sītā (SS2).

शिष्या (*śiṣyā*) F. "worth teaching or instructing", Bhavānī (BS). **शिष्य** (*śiṣya*) M.

शुचिका (*śucikā*) F. "she who speaks with purity or innocence", an Apsaras (MBh). **शुचिक** (*śucika*) M.

शुचिमान् (*śucimān*) M. "possessing purity and goodness", Viṣṇu (VS3). **शुचिमती** (*śucimatī*) F.

शुचिव्रत (*śucivrata*) M. "observing a vow of purity", a king (MBh). **शुचिव्रता** (*śucivratā*) F.

शुचिश्रवस् (*śuciśravas*) MF. "one whose fame is pure or bright",

Kṛṣṇa (MBh).

शुचिश्री (*śuciśrī*) F. "she whose *śrī* (affluence, prosperity, brilliance, success, etc.) is pure or bright", a queen (BrP).

शुभंयु (*śubhaṃyu*) MF. "auspicious, fortunate, desiring auspiciousness", used in ṚVŚ, BK.

शुभञ्जय (*śubhañjaya*) M. "conquering the bright or eminent ones", Narasiṃha (NS). **शुभञ्जया** (*śubhañjayā*) F.

शुभाक्ष (*śubhākṣa*) M. "with auspicious eyes", Śiva (ŚS1). **शुभाक्षी** (*śubhākṣī*) F.

शुभानन (*śubhānana*) M. "having an auspicious face, good-looking", Gaṇeśa (GS2). **शुभानना** (*śubhānanā*) F.

शुभावती (*śubhāvatī*) F. "possessing beauty or lustre", Gaṅgā (GS3), Sarasvatī (SS3). **शुभावान्** (*śubhāvān*) M.

शृञ्जय (*śṛñjaya*) M. "the conqueror of the violent", a king (VaP). **शृञ्जया** (*śṛñjayā*) F. a queen (VāP).

शैरीषी (*śairīṣī*) F. "associated with (resembling) the *śirīṣa* flower (*Albizia lebbeck*)", Rādhā (RS2). **शैरीष** (*śairīṣa*) M.

शैशिर (*śaiśira*) M. "devoted to *śiśira* (=Viṣṇu as per VS1)", a *ṛṣi* (MaP). **शैशिरी** (*śaiśirī*) F.

शोभावती (*śobhāvatī*) F. "possessing beauty or lustre", Durgā (DS4), Gaṅgā (GS3), Gāyatrī (GS4). **शोभावान्** (*śobhāvān*) M.

श्रविष्ठ (*śraviṣṭha*) M. "most famous", a star (BrP). **श्रविष्ठा** (*śraviṣṭhā*) F. a princess (BrP).

श्रित (*śrita*) M. "served, honoured", Hanumān (HS). **श्रिता** (*śritā*) F.

श्रीकरी (*śrīkarī*) F. "causing *śrī* (affluence, prosperity, abundance, opulence, brilliance, fame, growth, success, etc.)", Annapūrṇā (AS), Durgā (DS3), Lalitā (LS1), . **श्रीकर** (*śrīkara*) M. Viṣṇu (VS1).

श्रीद (*śrīda*) M. "the bestower of *śrī*", Viṣṇu (VS1), Rāma (RS1), Kṛṣṇa (KS1), Hanumān (HS). **श्रीदा** (*śrīdā*) F. Annapūrṇā (AS).

श्रीप्रदा (*śrīpradā*) F. "eminent bestower of *śrī*", Rādhā (RS2). **श्रीप्रद** (*śrīprada*) M.

श्रीमयी (*śrīmayī*) F. "full of (=rich in) *śrī*", Annapūrṇā (AS), Sarasvatī (SS3). **श्रीमय** (*śrīmaya*) M. Viṣṇu (VS2).

श्रीयुता (*śrīyutā*) F. "endowed with *śrī*", Durgā (DS3). **श्रीयुत** (*śrīyuta*) M.

श्रीवर (*śrīvara*) M. "the husband of Śrī = Lakṣmī", Narasiṃha (NS).

श्रीविजया (*śrīvijayā*) F. "she whose victory is auspicious", Lalitā (BrP). **श्रीविजय** (*śrīvijaya*) M.

श्रीशिवा (*śrīśivā*) F. "Śivā who is endowed with *śrī*", Lalitā (LS1). **श्रीशिव** (*śrīśiva*) M.

श्रुतकर्मा (*śrutakarmā*) MF. "one whose acts are famous", son of Sahadeva (MBh).

श्रुतञ्जय (*śrutañjaya*) M. "the conqueror of the renowned", a king (BhP). **श्रुतञ्जया** (*śrutañjayā*) F.

श्रुतदेव (*śrutadeva*) M. "like a god in knowledge", son of Kṛṣṇa (BhP). **श्रुतदेवी** (*śrutadevī*) F.

श्रुतर्षि (*śrutarṣi*) M. "a *ṛṣi* distinguished by knowledge", (BrP, VāP).

श्रुतश्रवस् (*śrutaśravas*) MF. "one whose fame is heard [all around], renowned", a *ṛṣi* (MBh).

श्रुतानीक (*śrutānīka*) M. "he whose army is famous", a king (MBh). **श्रुतानीका** (*śrutānīkā*) F.

श्रुतायुस् (*śrutāyus*) MF. "one whose age (=life) is famous", a king (MBh).

श्रुतिमान् (*śrutimān*) M. "he whose ears are praiseworthy, he who is always with *śrutis* (Vedas)", Śiva (ŚS3), Sūrya (SS1), Kṛṣṇa (KS1). **श्रुतिमती** (*śrutimatī*) F.

श्रेयस्क (*śreyaska*) M. "he who sounds (=speaks) for well-being", Dattātreya (DS2). **श्रेयस्का** (*śreyaskā*) F.

श्रेयस्कर (*śreyaskara*) M. "causing welfare, happiness", Sūrya (SS1). **श्रेयस्करी** (*śreyaskarī*) F.

श्रोतव्या (*śrotavyā*) F. "worth listening to", Lakṣmī (LS3). **श्रोतव्य** (*śrotavya*) M.

श्लाघ्य (*ślāghya*) M. "deserving praise, praiseworthy", Viṣṇu (VS2). **श्लाघ्या** (*ślāghyā*) F.

श्लोक्य (*ślokya*) M. "praiseworthy, renowned", Kṛṣṇa (RKS).

श्लोक्या (*ślokyā*) F.

श्वाजित (*śvājita*) M. "unconquered by the dogs [of Yama]", a *ṛṣi* (BrP). **श्वाजिता** (*śvājitā*) F.

श्वेतकेतु (*śvetaketu*) MF. "having a white flag", a *ṛṣi* (MBh).

षडानन (*ṣaḍānana*) M. "having six heads", Skanda (BrP, VāP).

षोडशी (*ṣoḍaśī*) F. "the sixteenth [kalā of Candra or the moon]", Durgā (DS3), Kālī (KS3).

संयमनी (*saṃyamanī*) F. "self-restrained, restraining, ruler", Yamunā (YS). **संयमन** (*saṃyamana*) M.

संयाति (*saṃyāti*) MF. "one who moves with others", son of Nahuṣa (MBh).

संयोगी (*saṃyogī*) M. "he whose nature is to join [actions with their fruits] properly", Śiva (ŚS3). **संयोगिनी** (*saṃyoginī*) F.

संवत्सर (*saṃvatsara*) M. "where everything is firmly located", Viṣṇu (VS1), Śiva (ŚS1).

संवर्तक (*saṃvartaka*) M. "destroying [everything at *pralaya*], the *pralaya* fire", son of Manyumān Agni (VāP). **संवर्तकी** (*saṃvartakī*) F.

संवृत (*saṃvṛta*) M. "hidden or concealed [by *avidyā*], secured", Viṣṇu (VS1), Śiva (ŚS3). **संवृता** (*saṃvṛtā*) F.

संवेद्य (*saṃvedya*) M. "worth knowing well", Kṛṣṇa (KS2). **संवेद्या** (*saṃvedyā*) F.

संश्रुत (*saṃśruta*) M. "well-heard, learned, knowledgeable", a *ṛṣi* (MaP). **संश्रुता** (*saṃśrutā*) F.

संहूति (*saṃhūti*) F. "calling or inviting together", wife of Agni (VāP).

सकल्प (*sakalpa*) M. "with *kalpa* (the *vedāṅga* prescribing ceremonial rules)", Śiva (ŚS1). **सकल्पा** (*sakalpā*) F.

सक्षमा (*sakṣamā*) F. "capable, with capacity". **सक्षम** (*sakṣama*) M.

सङ्क्रन्दन (*saṅkrandana*) M. "he who makes [his enemies] cry", Indra (AK). **सङ्क्रन्दना** (*saṅkrandanā*) F.

सत्कर्मा (*satkarmā*) MF. "one whose actions are good or true", a king (BhP).

सत्कीर्ति (*satkīrti*) MF. "possessing true fame, well-known", Bhavānī (BS).

सत्कृत (*satkṛta*) M. "worshipped, respected", Viṣṇu (VS1). **सत्कृता** (*satkṛtā*) F.

सत्कृति (*satkṛti*) MF. "righteous, performing good or noble acts", Bhavānī (BS), a king (BhP).

सत्त्वात्मा (*sattvātmā*) M. "having the nature of *sattva*, one whose *ātman* (=mind) dwells in *sattva*", Dattātreya (DS2).

सत्यकर्मा (*satyakarmā*) MF. "one whose actions are true or for truth", a king (VāP, ViP).

सत्यकेतु (*satyaketu*) MF. "with the banner of truth", Hanumān

(HS).

सत्यमित्र (*satyamitra*) M. "a friend of truth", one of the *Maruts* (VāP). **सत्यमित्रा** (*satyamitrā*) F.

सत्यमेधस् (*satyamedhas*) MF. "possessing a truthful intellect", Viṣṇu (VS1).

सत्यम्भरा (*satyambharā*) F. "nourishing or supporting truth", a river (BhP). **सत्यम्भर** (*satyambhara*) M.

सत्यरता (*satyaratā*) F. "engrossed in (=devoted to) truth", a princess (BrP, VāP). **सत्यरत** (*satyarata*) M.

सत्यरथ (*satyaratha*) M. "having the chariot of truth, fighting by means of truth", a king (BhP). **सत्यरथा** (*satyarathā*) F.

सत्यवाक् (*satyavāk*) MF. "speaking the truth", son of Cākṣuṣa Manu (BrP, VāP).

सत्यवास (*satyavāsa*) M. "the abode of truth", Rāma (RS1). **सत्यवासा** (*satyavāsā*) F.

सत्यश्रवस् (*satyaśravas*) MF. "one whose fame is true, having true fame", a king (BhP).

सत्यसेन (*satyasena*) M. "he whose army is truth [alone], fighting by means of truth", *avatāra* of Viṣṇu in third *manvantara* (BhP). **सत्यसेना** (*satyasenā*) F.

सत्यहित (*satyahita*) M. "beneficial for truth", a king (BhP). **सत्यहिता** (*satyahitā*) F.

सत्यायुस् (*satyāyus*) MF. "one whose age (=life) is devoted to truth", son of Purūravas (BhP).

सत्येयु (*satyeyu*) MF. "desirous of truth", son of Raudrāśva (BhP).

सत्वरा (*satvarā*) F. "swift, quick [to act]", Bhavānī (BS). **सत्वर** (*satvara*) M.

सदसस्पति (*sadasaspati*) M. "lord of the assembly", one of the Rudras (VāP).

सद्गति (*sadgati*) MF. "having a good or true path or way", Bhavānī (BS).

सद्भाव (*sadbhāva*) M. "he whose nature is good or true", Viṣṇu (VS2). **सद्भावा** (*sadbhāvā*) F.

सद्भूति (*sadbhūti*) MF. "with a good or true existence", Bhavānī (BS).

सनद्वाज (*sanadvāja*) M. "acquiring wealth or power", a king (BhP).

सनातनी (*sanātanī*) F. "eternal, permanent", Yamunā (YS), Lakṣmī (LS2), Bhavānī (BS). **सनातन** (*sanātana*) M.

सन्धाता (*sandhātā*) M. "he who joins or connects", Narasiṃha (NS). **सन्धात्री** (*sandhātrī*) F.

सन्धिनी (*sandhinī*) F. "she who has [praiseworthy] unions or alliances", Lakṣmī (LS2). **सन्धी** (*sandhī*) M.

सन्धिमान् (*sandhimān*) M. "he whose *sandhis* (alliances) are praiseworthy", Viṣṇu (VS1). **सन्धिमती** (*sandhimatī*) F.

सन्नति (*sannati*) MF. "one who shows modesty or humility for the noble", Durgā (DS3), a king (BrP, VāP, ViP).

सन्नतेयु (*sannateyu*) MF. "wishing to revere", son of Raudrāśva (BhP).

सप्तसप्ति (*saptasapti*) M. "having seven horses", Sūrya (SS1).

सप्तार्चिस् (*saptārcis*) M. "having seven flames", Agni (AK), Sūrya (SS1).

सप्ताश्व (*saptāśva*) M. "having seven horses", Sūrya (SS1).

सप्तिमान् (*saptimān*) M. "having praiseworthy horses", Sūrya (SS1). **सप्तिमती** (*saptimatī*) F.

सप्रमोद (*sapramoda*) M. "with great happiness or delight, eminently blissful", Gaṇeśa (GS2). **सप्रमोदा** (*sapramodā*) F.

सभावान् (*sabhāvān*) M. "present in a council or assembly (=suitable for an assembly)", used for *yajña* (ṚVŚ). **सभावती** (*sabhāvatī*) F.

समञ्जस (*samañjasa*) M. "proper, correct, virtuous", Rāma (RS1). **समञ्जसा** (*samañjasā*) F.

समर-मर्दन (*samara-mardana*) M. "destroying [the enemies] in a battle", Śiva (ŚS1). **समर-मर्दनी** (*samara-mardanī*) F.

समात्मा (*samātmā*) M. "with an equanimous *ātman* (=mind)", Viṣṇu (VS1), Rāma (RS1).

समाम्नाय (*samāmnāya*) M. "[having the form of] the Vedas", Śiva (ŚS1).

समायुक्त (*samāyukta*) M. "connected, united, prepared", Sūrya (SS1). **समायुक्ता** (*samāyuktā*) F.

समावर्त (*samāvarta*) M. "rotating well [the wheel of time or the universe]", Viṣṇu (VS1). **समावर्ता** (*samāvartā*) F.

समितिञ्जय (*samitiñjaya*) M. "conqueror of battles", Viṣṇu (VS1), Sūrya (SS1), Narasiṃha (NS). **समितिञ्जया** (*samitiñjayā*) F.

समीची (*samīcī*) F. "she who accompanies or goes with [the noble], the best, foremost, correct, accurate", an Apsaras (MaP). **सम्यङ्** (*samyaṅ*) M.

समीरज (*samīraja*) M. "son of Vāyu", Hanumān (HS).

समुद्रप (*samudrapa*) M. "he who drank the ocean", Agastya (BrP).

सम्भाव्य (*sambhāvya*) M. "worthy of being well-honoured, to be well-regarded", Śiva (ŚS3). **सम्भाव्या** (*sambhāvyā*) F.

सम्भूति (*sambhūti*) MF. "having complete existence, powers, or capabilities", a queen (BhP).

सरिद्वरा (*saridvarā*) F. "the best among the rivers", Gaṅgā (GS3).

सर्वग (*sarvaga*) M. "omnipresent, going everywhere", Viṣṇu (VS1), Śiva (ŚS1), Sūrya (SS1), Rāma (RS1). **सर्वगा** (*sarvagā*) F. Lakṣmī (LS2), Rādhā (RS2), Lalitā (LS1).

सर्वद (*sarvada*) M. "bestowing everything", Śiva (ŚS1), Sūrya

(SS1). **सर्वदा** (*sarvadā*) F. Lakṣmī (LS3), Pārvatī (PS), Sītā (SS2).

सर्वदृक् (*sarvadṛk*) MF. "seeing everything, omniscient", Viṣṇu (VS1), Rāma (RS1).

सर्वमयी (*sarvamayī*) F. "consisting of everything, all-pervading", Lakṣmī (LS2), Lalitā (LS1). **सर्वमय** (*sarvamaya*) M. Dattātreya (DS2).

सर्वमित्र (*sarvamitra*) M. "friend to one and all", Viṣṇu (VS3). **सर्वमित्रा** (*sarvamitrā*) F.

सर्ववित्/सर्वविद् (*sarvavit/sarvavid*) MF. "one who knows everything, omniscient", Viṣṇu (VS3).

सर्वाक्ष (*sarvākṣa*) M. "he whose eyes see everything, omniscient", Viṣṇu (VS2). **सर्वाक्षी** (*sarvākṣī*) F.

सर्वागम (*sarvāgama*) M. "the origin of everything", Kṛṣṇa (KS1). **सर्वागमा** (*sarvāgamā*) F.

सर्वात्मा (*sarvātmā*) M. "the *ātman* of everybody [as the *antaryāmin*]", Sūrya (SS1), Rāma (RS1), Kṛṣṇa (KS1).

सर्वादि (*sarvādi*) M. "the origin of everything", Viṣṇu (VS1), Rāma (RS1).

सर्वाद्य (*sarvādya*) M. "the first one, primeval", Viṣṇu (VS3). **सर्वाद्या** (*sarvādyā*) F.

सर्वायुध (*sarvāyudha*) M. "having all weapons, the source of all weapons", Śiva (ŚS1). **सर्वायुधा** (*sarvāyudhā*) F.

सर्वाशय (*sarvāśaya*) M. "the resting place of everything", Śiva (ŚS1). **सर्वाशया** (*sarvāśayā*) F.

सर्वेशी (*sarveśī*) F. "the goddess of everything", a *yoginī śakti* (BrP). **सर्वेश** (*sarveśa*) M.

सहस्रजित् (*sahasrajit*) MF. "one who conquers thousands (=uncountably many)", son of Kṛṣṇa (BhP).

सहस्रनामा (*sahasranāmā*) M. "he who has thousands of names", Viṣṇu (VS2). **सहस्रनाम्नी** (*sahasranāmnī*) F.

सहस्रपात् (*sahasrapāt*) MF. "one who has a thousand (=uncountably many) feet, i.e. one who can go everywhere", Viṣṇu (VS1), Śiva (ŚS1).

सहस्राक्ष (*sahasrākṣa*) M. "having a thousand (=uncountably many) eyes, seeing everything", Viṣṇu (VS1), Śiva (ŚS1). **सहस्राक्षी** (*sahasrākṣī*) F. Bhavānī (BS), Lalitā (LS1), Sītā (SS2).

सहस्रार्चिस् (*sahasrārcis*) MF. "with thousands of (=infinite) rays", Viṣṇu (VS1).

सहोजित् (*sahojit*) MF. "one who conquers [others'] strength or [others] with strength", used for Indra (AVP).

साक्षिणी (*sākṣiṇī*) F. "she who sees or observes", Bhavānī (BS). **साक्षी** (*sākṣī*) M. Viṣṇu (VS1).

सात्त्विकी (*sāttvikī*) F. "endowed with *sattva*, true, wise, noble, excellent, reverential, resolute, respectable, pure, strong, full of life, conscious", Bhavānī (BS). **सात्त्विक** (*sāttvika*) M.

सात्वत (*sātvata*) M. "possessing *sat* (existence or truth)", Kṛṣṇa (MBh), Viṣṇu (TK). **सात्वती** (*sātvatī*) F.

साध्य (*sādhya*) M. "he who is worth reaching (=knowing), he who can be reached [by anybody]", Viṣṇu (VS2). **साध्या** (*sādhyā*) F. Lakṣmī (LS2), Durgā (DS3).

सामग (*sāmaga*) M. "singer of Sāmaveda, he who is reached (=understood or known) by the Sāmaveda", Viṣṇu (VS1), Sūrya (SS1). **सामगा** (*sāmagā*) F.

सामगेय (*sāmageya*) M. "sung (glorified) by *sāmans* (mantras of the Sāmaveda)", Rāma (RS1). **सामगेया** (*sāmageyā*) F.

सामस्वन (*sāmasvana*) M. "with an appeasing or soothing sound", Narasiṃha (NS). **सामस्वना** (*sāmasvanā*) F.

सामिधेनी (*sāmidhenī*) F. "kindling the firewood of *yajña*", Bhavānī (BS). **सामिधेन्य** (*sāmidhenya*) M.

सारस्वत (*sārasvata*) M. "eloquent, worshipper of Sarasvatī", Narasiṃha (NS). **सारस्वती** (*sārasvatī*) F.

सारा (*sārā*) F. "strong or powerful", epithet of Durgā (DSS). **सार** (*sāra*) M. Śiva (ŚS3).

सार्वभौम (*sārvabhauma*) M. "the universal king or emperor", Kṛṣṇa (KS2), Hanumān (HS). **सार्वभौमी** (*sārvabhaumī*) F.

सावर्णि (*sāvarṇi*) M. "son of Savarṇā", the eighth Manu (BhP).

सिद्धिदा (*siddhidā*) F. "she who gives success", Bhavānī (BS). **सिद्धिद** (*siddhida*) M.

सीरायुध (*sīrāyudha*) M. "having the plough as his weapon", Balarāma (ViP).

सुकर्म/सुकर्मा (*sukarma/sukarmā*) M. "he whose actions are good", Narasiṃha (NS). **सुकर्मा** (*sukarmā*) F.

सुकर्ष (*sukarṣa*) M. "very attractive", a *mantragaṇa* (MaP). **सुकर्षा** (*sukarṣā*) F.

सुकुला (*sukulā*) F. "having a good or noble family", Bhavānī (BS). **सुकुल** (*sukula*) M.

सुकेतन (*suketana*) M. "with a good sign or body (form)", Sūrya (SS1). **सुकेतना** (*suketanā*) F.

सुक्षत्र (*sukṣatra*) M. "ruling well, having a good kingdom, powerful", a king (MBh, BrP). **सुक्षत्रा** (*sukṣatrā*) F.

सुगायन (*sugāyana*) M. "singing well", Kṛṣṇa (KS1). **सुगायनी** (*sugāyanī*) F.

सुगीति (*sugīti*) MF. "one who sings well, the object of good (pious) songs (hymns)", Bhavānī (BS).

सुगृहा (*sugṛhā*) F. "she whose abode is beautiful, she who makes the homes beautiful", Lakṣmī (LS3). **सुगृह** (*sugṛha*) M.

सुगोत्रा (*sugotrā*) F. "the good protectress of *go* (cows or speech)", Bhavānī (BS). **सुगोत्र** (*sugotra*) M.

सुगोपी (*sugopī*) F. "the good cowherdess", Rādhā (RS2). **सुगोप** (*sugopa*) M.

सुघोर (*sughora*) M. "very frightening", Narasiṃha (NS). **सुघोरा**

(*sughorā*) F.

सुचक्षुस् (*sucakṣus*) MF. "having beautiful eyes, seeing (=knowing) well, wise or learned", a river (BrP).

सुजन्मा (*sujanmā*) MF. "having a noble or auspicious birth", Bhavānī (BS).

सुतन्तु (*sutantu*) MF. "with a beautiful expanse or thread (=the extended universe)", Viṣṇu (VS1), Bhavānī (BS).

सुतापि (*sutāpi*) M. "coming from one whose austerities are severe", an *avatāra* in the second *Dvāpara* (VāP). **सुतापी** (*sutāpī*) F. a daughter of Devakī (MaP).

सुतारा (*sutārā*) F. "very radiant or bright", Lakṣmī (LS2). **सुतार** (*sutāra*) M.

सुतारिणी (*sutāriṇī*) F. "she who enables to cross over [the worldly ocean]", Lakṣmī (LS2). **सुतारी** (*sutārī*) M.

सुदक्ष (*sudakṣa*) M. "very capable, strong, or clever", a *deva* (BrP). **सुदक्षा** (*sudakṣā*) F.

सुदती (*sudatī*) F. "having beautiful teeth", an Apsaras (BrP). **सुदन्** (*sudan*) M.

सुदीप्तिमान् (*sudīptimān*) M. "extremely brilliant or radiant", Rāma (RS1). **सुदीप्तिमती** (*sudīptimatī*) F.

सुद्यु (*sudyu*) MF. "very bright, brilliant", a king (BhP).

सुद्युम्ना (*sudyumnā*) F. "with good (=benevolent) *dyumna* (=splendour, glory, lustre, power, opulence, or inspiration)",

Sītā (SS2). सुद्युम्न (*sudyumna*) M.

सुद्विजा (*sudvijā*) F. "she who has beautiful teeth", Yamunā (YS). सुद्विज (*sudvija*) M.

सुनामा (*sunāmā*) MF. "well-named, having a good name (=fame)", son of Devakī and Vasudeva (BrP), son of Garuḍa (MBh), used for Devakī (VāP). सुनाम्नी (*sunāmnī*) F. wife of Vasudeva (BrP).

सुनिर्मला (*sunirmalā*) F. "very clean or pure", Lakṣmī (LS2). सुनिर्मल (*sunirmala*) M.

सुनिश्चल (*suniścala*) M. "extremely firm", Śiva (ŚS1). सुनिश्चला (*suniścalā*) F.

सुपक्ष (*supakṣa*) M. "having good friends, arguing well", a *deva* (VāP). सुपक्षा (*supakṣā*) F.

सुपथ्या (*supathyā*) F. "very suitable or proper", Bhavānī (BS). सुपथ्य (*supathya*) M.

सुपर्वा (*suparvā*) MF. "having good joints or festivals, a deity", Bhavānī (BS).

सुपुष्पा (*supuṣpā*) F. "having (=adorned with) beautiful flowers", Lakṣmī (LS2). सुपुष्प (*supuṣpa*) M.

सुपोषा (*supoṣā*) F. "nourishing well", Lakṣmī (LS3). सुपोष (*supoṣa*) M.

सुप्रताप (*supratāpa*) M. "very hot, radiant, majestic, or heroic", Sūrya (SS1). सुप्रतापा (*supratāpā*) F.

सुप्रतिष्ठा (*supratiṣṭhā*) F. "well-established, very firm, very famous", Lalitā (LS1). **सुप्रतिष्ठ** (*supratiṣṭha*) M.

सुप्रभाव (*suprabhāva*) M. "very powerful, dignified, or majestic", Sūrya (SS1). **सुप्रभावा** (*suprabhāvā*) F.

सुबन्धु (*subandhu*) M. "having good friends", name of a *vānara* (BrP).

सुबीज (*subīja*) M. "having good (= fruitful) seed, he whose *bīja* (mystical sound in a mantra) is good, the good cause [of the everything]", Śiva (ŚS1). **सुबीजा** (*subījā*) F.

सुभगा (*subhagā*) F. "prosperous, beautiful, delicate", Gaṅgā (GS3), Lalitā (LS1), Bhavānī (BS). **सुभग** (*subhaga*) M.

सुभद्रिका (*subhadrikā*) F. "very auspicious, beautiful, or virtuous", Rādhā (RKS). **सुभद्रक** (*subhadraka*) M.

सुभाषण (*subhāṣaṇa*) M. "speaking well", a king (BhP). **सुभाषणा** (*subhāṣaṇā*) F.

सुभुज (*subhuja*) M. "with handsome arms", Viṣṇu (VS1), Rāma (RS1). **सुभुजा** (*subhujā*) F.

सुमन्तु (*sumantu*) MF. "advising well", a *ṛṣi* and disciple of Vyāsa (BhP).

सुमहस् (*sumahas*) MF. "excellent, glorious, with a brilliant lustre", Durgā (DS3).

सुमूर्ति (*sumūrti*) MF. "having a good form", Sūrya (SS1), Sītā (SS2), Pārvatī (PS).

सुयज्ञ (*suyajña*) M. "he whose *yajñas* are great", an *avatāra* of Viṣṇu (BhP). **सुयज्ञा** (*suyajñā*) F.

सुयन्त्रा (*suyantrā*) F. "possessing a beautiful *yantra*", Lakṣmī (LS2). **सुयन्त्र** (*suyantra*) M.

सुयामुन (*suyāmuna*) M. "he who is the cause of *yāmuna* (the water of Yamunā) being pure", Viṣṇu (VS1).

सुयुक्त (*suyukta*) M. "very correct or right, very auspicious, well-endowed", Śiva (ŚS1). **सुयुक्ता** (*suyuktā*) F.

सुरश्मि (*suraśmi*) MF. "having beautiful rays or eyelashes", used for Soma (ṚVŚ).

सुरार्चित (*surārcita*) M. "worshipped by the gods", Rāma (RS1). **सुरार्चिता** (*surārcitā*) F. Sītā (SS2).

सुरूप (*surūpa*) M. "handsome, wise", Śiva (ŚS1). **सुरूपा** (*surūpā*) F.

सुरेज्या (*surejyā*) F. "worthy of being honoured by the *suras* (gods)", Tulasī (VK1). **सुरेज्य** (*surejya*) M.

सुरोत्तम (*surottama*) M. "the best among the *suras* (gods)", Viṣṇu (VS2), Kṛṣṇa (MBh). **सुरोत्तमा** (*surottamā*) F. Bhavānī (BS).

सुलक्ष्मणा (*sulakṣmaṇā*) F. "possessing auspicious marks or signs", Rādhā (RS2). **सुलक्ष्मण** (*sulakṣmaṇa*) M.

सुवर्चस् (*suvarcas*) MF. "possessing great power or splendour, very powerful or brilliant", Durgā (DS3), son of Sāvarṇa Manu

(BrP), son of Garuḍa (MBh), daughter of Sāraṇa (VāP).

सुवस्त्रा (*suvastrā*) F. "well-clothed, brightly dressed", Bhavānī (BS). **सुवस्त्र** (*suvastra*) M.

सुवाक् (*suvāk*) MF. "with a beautiful speech, praiseworthy, having a mellifluous voice or speech", Sūrya (SS1), a *ṛṣi* (VāP).

सुवासा (*suvāsā*) F. "having a beautiful abode or fragrance", Lakṣmī (LS3). **सुवास** (*suvāsa*) M.

सुविक्रम (*suvikrama*) M. "very courageous, valorous, or brave", Rāma (RS1), Kṛṣṇa (KS2). **सुविक्रमा** (*suvikramā*) F.

सुविभु (*suvibhu*) MF. "very powerful, great, strong, effective, or capable", a king (BrP).

सुविश्रुता (*suviśrutā*) F. "very famous, very well-known", Rādhā (RKS). **सुविश्रुत** (*suviśruta*) M.

सुवृता (*suvṛtā*) F. "well-surrounded (=well-served), well-covered (=well-adorned)", Durgā (DS4). **सुवृत** (*suvṛta*) M.

सुवृष्टि (*suvṛṣṭi*) F. "the source of good rains", Bhavānī (BS).

सुवेणी (*suveṇī*) F. "having a beautiful braid", Bhavānī (BS).

सुवेध (*suvedha*) M. "piercing well", Narasiṃha (NS). **सुवेधा** (*suvedhā*) F.

सुव्यूहा (*suvyūhā*) F. "with good manifestations", Bhavānī (BS). **सुव्यूह** (*suvyūha*) M.

सुशर्मा (*suśarmā*) MF. "very happy", Narasiṃha (NS).

सुशाख (*suśākha*) M. "with beautiful limbs or *śākhās* [of Vedas]", Narasiṃha (NS). **सुशाखा** (*suśākhā*) F.

सुशारद (*suśārada*) M. "with good (= pleasant) speech", Śiva (ŚS1). **सुशारदा** (*suśāradā*) F.

सुशुद्धा (*suśuddhā*) F. "very pure, chaste, or bright", Lakṣmī (LS2). **सुशुद्ध** (*suśuddha*) M.

सुशोभना (*suśobhanā*) F. "very beautiful or resplendent", Sītā (SS2). **सुशोभन** (*suśobhana*) M.

सुशोभा (*suśobhā*) F. "very bright or beautiful", Yamunā (YS). **सुशोभ** (*suśobha*) M.

सुश्रद्धा (*suśraddhā*) F. "very faithful or believing, possessing a lot of *śraddhā*", Bhavānī (BS). **सुश्रद्ध** (*suśraddha*) M.

सुश्रवस् (*suśravas*) MF. "of great renown", a Prajāpati (VāP).

सुश्रीक (*suśrīka*) M. "he whose *śrī* (radiance, grace, prosperity, intelligence, etc.) is magnificent or abundant", used to describe a hero or a protagonist in SD. **सुश्रीका** (*suśrīkā*) F.

सुश्लोक (*suśloka*) M. "well-renowned, very famous", Kṛṣṇa (RKS). **सुश्लोका** (*suślokā*) F.

सुसौम्या (*susaumyā*) F. "very lovely or gentle", Sītā (SS2). **सुसौम्य** (*susaumya*) M.

सुस्थिर (*susthira*) M. "very firm, steady, or stable", Kṛṣṇa (KS1). **सुस्थिरा** (*susthirā*) F.

सुस्पृहा (*suspṛhā*) F. "having good wishes", Bhavānī (BS). **सुस्पृह**

(*susprha*) M.

सुस्मृति (*susmṛti*) MF. "having a good memory, remembering well", Bhavānī (BS).

सुस्वप्न (*susvapna*) M. "having good dreams, the *vibhu* of *svapna* (*taijasa*)", Śiva (ŚS1). सुस्वप्ना (*susvapnā*) F.

सुहोत्र (*suhotra*) M. "with good offerings [for Agni]", a king (MBh). सुहोत्रा (*suhotrā*) F.

सूर्यजा (*sūryajā*) F. "daughter of Sūrya", Yamunā (YS). सूर्यज (*sūryaja*) M.

सेतुकृत् (*setukṛt*) MF. "the creator of the bridge", Hanumān (HS).

सेनजित् (*senajit*) MF. "conquering an army", used in ŚYM.

सेनाजित् (*senājit*) MF. "conquering an army", a king (MBh).

सेव्या (*sevyā*) F. "worthy of being served or waited upon", Rādhā (RKS), Gaṅgā (GS3), Yamunā (YS), Lakṣmī (LS2), Rādhā (RS2). सेव्य (*sevya*) M. Rāma (RS1).

सोमप (*somapa*) M. "the drinker of *soma*", Viṣṇu (VS1), Narasiṃha (NS). सोमपा (*somapā*) F. Lakṣmī (LS2).

सोमाधि (*somādhi*) M. "hoping for *soma*", king (MaP, VāP).

सोमापि (*somāpi*) M. "a friend of *soma* (the moon or the wind)", a king (BhP).

सौमित्रि (*saumitri*) M. "the son of Sumitrā", Lakṣmaṇa (MBh).

सौम्यदात्री (*saumyadātrī*) F. "the bestower of gentleness", Rādhā (RS2). **सौम्यदाता** (*saumyadātā*) M.

स्कन्दसू (*skandasū*) F. "the mother of Skanda (Kārttikeya)", Gaṅgā (GS3).

स्तव्य (*stavya*) M. "fit to be praised, praiseworthy", Viṣṇu (VS1), Rāma (RS1). **स्तव्या** (*stavyā*) F.

स्तुत्य (*stutya*) M. "worth praising, praiseworthy, laudable", Narasiṃha (NS), Hanumān (HS). **स्तुत्या** (*stutyā*) F. Gaṅgā (GS3).

स्तोभित (*stobhita*) M. "encouraged, praised by *stobhas* (sounds in Sāmaveda)", used for Kṛṣṇa (BhP). **स्तोभिता** (*stobhitā*) F.

स्थलेयु (*sthaleyu*) MF. "desiring land or place", a king (VāP).

स्थलेश (*sthaleśa*) M. "lord of the lands", Narasiṃha (NS). **स्थलेशी** (*sthaleśī*) F.

स्थविर (*sthavira*) M. "firm, steady, ancient", Viṣṇu (VS1), Sūrya (SS1). **स्थविरा** (*sthavirā*) F.

स्थविष्ठ (*sthaviṣṭha*) M. "greatest, strongest, largest", Viṣṇu (VS1), Rāma (RS1). **स्थविष्ठा** (*sthaviṣṭhā*) F.

स्थाणु (*sthāṇu*) MF. "firm, steady, stable", Viṣṇu (VS1), Śiva (ŚS1), Sūrya (SS1), Rāma (RS1), Dattātreya (DS2).

स्थावरा (*sthāvarā*) F. "fixed, immovable, eternal", Bhavānī (BS). **स्थावर** (*sthāvara*) M.

स्थिर (*sthira*) M. "stationary, firm, stable, still, everlasting",

Śiva (ŚS1). **स्थिरा** (*sthirā*) F. Lakṣmī (LS2).

स्थेय (*stheya*) M. "the judge (=the witness of all actions)", Sūrya (SS1). **स्थेया** (*stheyā*) F.

स्नेहला (*snehalā*) F. "full of love, fond of", the right name to use for a girl in place of Snehal (*snehala*). **स्नेहल** (*snehala*) M.

स्मय (*smaya*) M. "smiling, he who smiles", a Prajāpati (MaP). **स्मया** (*smayā*) F.

स्मितास्या (*smitāsyā*) F. "having a smiling face", Bhavānī (BS). **स्मितास्य** (*smitāsya*) M.

स्मृतिमान् (*smṛtimān*) M. "having an excellent memory", Rāma (RS1). **स्मृतिमती** (*smṛtimatī*) F.

स्रग्विणी (*sragviṇī*) F. "wearing a garland [of flowers]", Yamunā (YS), Sītā (SS2). **स्रग्वी** (*sragvī*) M. Viṣṇu (VS1), Rāma (RS1).

स्वक्ष (*svakṣa*) M. "he who has beautiful eyes (*akṣis*), he who has beautiful sense organs (*akṣas*)", Viṣṇu (VS1). **स्वक्षा** (*svakṣā*) F. Kālī (KS3), Yamunā (YS). Note: **स्वक्षा** (*svakṣā*) means "she who has beautiful sense organs (*akṣas*)" while **स्वक्षी** (*svakṣī*) means "she who has beautiful eyes (*akṣis*)".

स्वधृत (*svadhṛta*) M. "held or restrained by himself, not held or restrained by anybody else", Viṣṇu (VS1), Śiva (ŚS3). **स्वधृता** (*svadhṛtā*) F.

स्वनय (*svanaya*) M. "he who is led by himself", a prince (ṚVŚ). **स्वनया** (*svanayā*) F.

स्वप्रकाशा (*svaprakāśā*) F. "self-luminous", Lalitā (LS1). **स्वप्रकाश** (*svaprakāśa*) M.

स्वप्रिया (*svapriyā*) F. "dear to *sva* (wealth, oneself, or those who are one's own)", Lakṣmī (LS3). **स्वप्रिय** (*svapriya*) M.

स्वभू (*svabhū*) MF. "self-existent, self-born", Rāma (RS1).

स्वयंतेजस् (*svayaṃtejas*) MF. "self-resplendent", Rāma (RS1).

स्वयंभू (*svayambhū*) M. "self-born, self-existing, uncreated", Viṣṇu (VS1), Śiva (ŚS1).

स्वरोचिस् (*svarocis*) MF. "self-resplendent, having his own brilliance", Agni (BhP), a king (MāP).

स्वर्गति (*svargati*) MF. "moving in *svarga*", Bhavānī (BS).

स्वर्गद (*svargada*) M. "he who grants *svarga*", Rāma (RS1). **स्वर्गदा** (*svargadā*) F.

स्वर्ग्या (*svargyā*) F. "belonging to *svarga*", Gaṅgā (GS3). **स्वर्ग्य** (*svargya*) M.

स्वर्णदी (*svarṇadī*) F. "the river of *svarga*", Yamunā (YS).

स्वर्धुनी (*svardhunī*) F. "the river in the sky or *svarga*", used for Gaṅgā (BhP).

स्वर्भानु (*svarbhānu*) M. "shining in the sky", Sūrya (SS1).

स्वर्मणि (*svarmaṇi*) MF. "the jewel of the sky", Yamunā (YS).

स्वर्यु (*svaryu*) MF. "one who makes [one] go to *svarloka* or *svarga*, one whose nature is to wish for *svar* (*svarga*, happiness, sky, splendour)", used for *stutis* in SVR.

स्वर्वित्/स्वर्विद् (*svarvit/svarvid*) MF. "one who knows or obtains *svar* (*svarga*, happiness, sky, splendour)", used many times in ṚVŚ.

स्ववश (*svavaśa*) M. "under his own control, not controlled or ruled by anybody else", Śiva (ŚS3). **स्ववशा** (*svavaśā*) F.

स्वश्रव (*svaśrava*) M. "having his own fame, renowned", a *ṛṣi* (MaP). **स्वश्रवा** (*svaśravā*) F.

स्वस्तिकृत् (*svastikṛt*) MF. "one who causes (= bestows) welfare and prosperity", Śiva (ŚS3).

स्वस्तिद (*svastida*) M. "the bestower of auspiciousness", Viṣṇu (VS1), Hanumān (HS). **स्वस्तिदा** (*svastidā*) F.

स्वस्तिमान् (*svastimān*) M. "blissful, auspicious", Hanumān (HS). **स्वस्तिमती** (*svastimatī*) F.

स्वारोचिष (*svārociṣa*) M. "son of *svarocis* (= Agni)", the second Manu (BhP). **स्वारोचिषी** (*svārociṣī*) F.

स्वास्य (*svāsya*) M. "with a handsome face", Viṣṇu (VS1). **स्वास्या** (*svāsyā*) F.

स्वोजस् (*svojas*) MF. "very strong, very powerful", Gaṇeśa (GS2).

हतारि (*hatāri*) MF. "one who has destroyed their enemies", Viṣṇu (VS2).

हयग (*hayaga*) M. "drawn by horses", Sūrya (SS1).

हरिग (*hariga*) M. "he who goes to or leads to Hari (Rāma or Vīṣṇu)", Hanumān (HS). **हरिगा** (*harigā*) F.

हरिणाक्ष (*hariṇākṣa*) M. "yellow-eyed, deer-eyed", Śiva (ŚS1). **हरिणाक्षी** (*hariṇākṣī*) F.

हरिताश्व (*haritāśva*) M. "having fallow horses", Sūrya (SS1).

हरिदश्व (*haridaśva*) M. "having fallow horses", Sūrya (SS1).

हरिभद्रा (*haribhadrā*) F. "she who is the cause of Hari's satisfaction", Lakṣmī (LS2). **हरिभद्र** (*haribhadra*) M.

हरिमेधस् (*harimedhas*) MF. "with the intelligence of Sūrya", father of Hari incarnation (BhP).

हरिवर्ष (*harivarṣa*) M. "showering rays of light, brilliant", son of Agnīdhra (BhP). **हरिवर्षा** (*harivarṣā*) F.

हर्यक्ष (*haryakṣa*) M. "lion, yellow-eyed, lion-eyed, he on whom Hari's eyes are fixed", Śiva (ŚS1). **हर्यक्षी** (*haryakṣī*) F.

हर्यश्व (*haryaśva*) M. "having tawny horses", Sūrya (SS1).

हलायुध (*halāyudha*) M. "he whose weapon is the plough (Balarāma)", Viṣṇu (VS1, VS2). **हलायुधा** (*halāyudhā*) F. Lakṣmī (LS2, LS3).

हविर्भुक् (*havirbhuk*) M. "he who consumes offerings", Agni (BrP, BhP).

हविर्भू (*havirbhū*) MF. "born from oblations, place of oblations", daughter of Kardama (BhP).

हविष्णु (*haviṣṇu*) MF. "offering oblations [to Agni in a yajña]", son of Aṅgiras (VāP).

हविष्मान् (*haviṣmān*) M. "possessing (=offering) oblations [to Agni]", a *ṛṣi* (BhP). **हविष्मती** (*haviṣmatī*) F. Kāmadhenu (BhP), daughter of Aṅgiras and Subhā (MBh).

हव्या (*havyā*) F. "worthy of being invoked", Durgā (DS3). **हव्य** (*havya*) M.

हस्तीश/हस्तीश्वर (*hastīśa/hastīśvara*) M. "the lord of the elephant", Śiva (ŚS1). **हस्तीशी/हस्तीश्वरी** (*hastīśī/hastīśvarī*) F.

हाटकी (*hāṭakī*) F. "golden, made of gold", a river (BhP).

हाटकेश (*hāṭakeśa*) M. "the lord of gold, a form of Śiva", similar to the name *hāṭakeśāna* of Mṛtyuñjaya (MS1). **हाटकेशी** (*hāṭakeśī*) F.

हुताग्नि (*hutāgni*) M. "he who offers oblations to Agni", a performer of *agnihotra* (MS2).

हुताशन (*hutāśana*) M. "eater of oblations", Agni (MBh).

हृदयालु (*hṛdayālu*) MF. "kind-hearted, affectionate", cited in PMB.

हृदिक (*hṛdika*) M. "kind-hearted", name of a king (BhP). **हृदिका** (*hṛdikā*) F.

हृद्देवी (*hṛddevī*) F. "goddess of the heart", a goddess (BrP). **हृद्देव** (*hṛddeva*) M.

हृद्यांशु (*hṛdyāṃśu*) MF. "having pleasant rays", the moon

(VK2).

हृल्लेखा (*hṛllekhā*) F. "the goddess of the heart", Lakṣmī (LS3).

हृषेयु (*hṛṣeyu*) MF. "desiring happiness", son of Bhadrāśva (MaP).

हेतुक (*hetuka*) M. "a logician, causing [something good]", a Bhairava (BrP). **हेतुका/हेतुकी** (*hetukā/hetukī*) F.

हेमकर (*hemakara*) M. "creator of [the *jāmbūnada*] gold", Śiva (ŚS1, ŚS5). **हेमकरी** (*hemakarī*) F.

हेमवान् (*hemavān*) M. "possessing [the brilliance of] gold", a mountain (MaP). **हेमवती** (*hemavatī*) F.

हेमाभा (*hemābhā*) F. "resembling gold, bright like gold", used for Sītā (VR). **हेमाभ** (*hemābha*) M.

होत्रक (*hotraka*) M. "assistant *hotṛ* (priest)", son of Kāñcana (BhP). **होत्रिका** (*hotrikā*) F.

होत्रिय (*hotriya*) M. "beneficial for *yajña*", Agni (BrP). **होत्रिया** (*hotriyā*) F.

ह्रीमती (*hrīmatī*) F. "modest", Lalitā (LS1). **ह्रीमान्** (*hrīmān*) M.

ह्लादिनी (*hlādinī*) F. "full of delight, delighting, pleasing", Lakṣmī (LS2). **ह्लादी** (*hlādī*) M.

Abbreviations

Note: There are two *Śiva-sahasranāmas* each in the *Liṅga-Purāṇa* and the *Mahābhārata*. In the below list, book and chapter numbers are shown only for the abbreviations used for these four *sahasranāmas* in order to distinguish them.

AgP	Agni-Purāṇa
AK	Amara-Koṣa
AS	Annapūrṇā-Sahasranāma (Rudrayāmala-Tantra)
AVP	Atharvaveda (Paippalāda-Saṃhitā)
AVŚ	Atharvaveda (Śaunaka-Saṃhitā)
BD	Bṛhaddevatā
BG	Bhagavad-Gītā
BhP	Śrīmadbhāgavata-Purāṇa
BK	Bhaṭṭikāvya
BrP	Brahmāṇḍa-Purāṇa
BVP	Brahmā-Vaivarta-Purāṇa
BS	Bhavānī-Sahasranāma (Rudrayāmala-Tantra)
DS1	Durgā-Sahasranāma (Kulārṇava-Tantra)
DS2	Dattātreya-Sahasranāma (Dattātreya-Purāṇa)
DS3	Durgā-Sahasranāma (Tantrarāja-Tantra)
DS4	Durgā-Sahasranāma (Skanda-Purāṇa)
DSS	Durgā-Saptaśatī (Mārkaṇḍeya-Purāṇa)
GS1	Gaṇeśa-Sahasranāma (Rudrayāmala-Tantra)

GS2	Gaṇeśa-Sahasranāma (Gaṇeśa-Tantra)
GS3	Gaṅgā-Sahasranāma (Skanda-Purāṇa)
GS4	Gāyatrī-Sahasranāma (Devībhāgavata-Purāṇa)
GS5	Gaṇeśa-Sahasranāma (Gaṇeśa-Purāṇa)
GS6	Go-Sahasranāma (Svāmī Rāmabhadrācārya)
HD	Haṃsadūta (Rūpa Gosvāmī)
HK	Halāyudha-Koṣa
HS	Hanumat-Sahasranāma (Mantra-Mahārṇava)
HV	Harivaṃśa
HYP	Haṭha-Yoga-Pradīpikā
Kāś	Kāśikā (commentary on Aṣṭādhyāyī)
KRM	Kṛdanta-Rūpa-Mālā
KS1	Kṛṣṇa-Sahasranāma (Viṣṇudharmottara-Purāṇa)
KS2	Kṛṣṇa-Sahasranāma (Sammohana-Tantra)
KS3	Kālī-Sahasranāma (Bṛhannīla-Tantra)
KS4	Kumārī-Sahasranāma (Rudrayāmala-Tantra)
KYM	Kṛṣṇa-Yajurveda (Maitrāyaṇī-Saṃhitā)
KYT	Kṛṣṇa-Yajurveda (Taittirīya-Saṃhitā)
LiP	Liṅga-Purāṇa
LS1	Lalitā-Sahasranāma (Brahmāṇḍa-Purāṇa)
LS2	Lakṣmī-Sahasranāma (Brahma-Purāṇa)
LS3	Lakṣmī-Sahasranāma (Skanda-Purāṇa)
LTS	Lalitā-Triśatī
MaP	Matsya-Purāṇa
MāP	Mārkaṇḍeya-Purāṇa
MBh	Mahābhārata
MK	Medinī-Koṣa

Abbreviations

MS1	Mṛtyuñjaya-Sahasranāma (Rudrayāmala-Tantra)
MS2	Manusmṛti
NS	Nṛsiṃha-Sahasranāma (Nṛsiṃha-Purāṇa)
PMB	Patañjali's Mahābhāṣya
PS	Pārvatī-Sahasranāma (Kūrma-Purāṇa)
RKS	Rādhā-Kṛṣṇa-Sahasranāma (Bṛhannāradīya-Purāṇa)
RS1	Rāma-Sahasranāma (Ānanda-Rāmāyaṇa)
RS2	Rādhikā-Sahasranāma (Nārada-Pāñcarātra)
ṚVŚ	Ṛgveda (Śākala-Saṃhitā)
SD	Sāhitya-Darpaṇa
SS1	Sūrya-Sahasranāma (Bhaviṣya-Purāṇa)
SS2	Sītā-Sahasranāma (Adbhuta-Rāmāyaṇa)
SS3	Sarasvatī-Sahasranāma (Skanda-Purāṇa)
SVR	Sāmaveda (Rāṇāyanīya-Saṃhitā)
ŚiP	Śiva-Purāṇa
ŚK	Śabdakalpadruma-Koṣa
ŚS1	Śiva-Sahasranāma (Mahābhārata 13.17)
ŚS2	Śiva-Sahasranāma (Śiva-Purāṇa)
ŚS3	Śiva-Sahasranāma (Liṅga-Purāṇa 1.98)
ŚS4	Śiva-Sahasranāma (Mahābhārata 12.284)
ŚS5	Śiva-Sahasranāma (Liṅga-Purāṇa 1.65)
ŚYM	Śukla-Yajurveda (Madhyāndina-Saṃhitā)
TK	Trikāṇḍaśeṣa-Koṣa
VāP	Vāyu-Purāṇa
ViP	Viṣṇu-Purāṇa
VK1	Vācaspatya-Koṣa
VK2	Vaijayantī-Koṣa

VR	Vālmīki-Rāmāyaṇa
VS1	Viṣṇu-Sahasranāma (Mahābhārata)
VS2	Viṣṇu-Sahasranāma (Nārada-Pāñcarātra)
VS3	Viṣṇu-Sahasranāma (Garuḍa-Purāṇa)
YS	Yamunā-Sahasranāma (Garga-Saṃhitā)